Best International Author

Mr. Johnson Mbabazi

Senior FRSPH

Understanding the Power of Love in the Emotional, Physical and Spiritual Realm:

The vast majority of both men and women now view romantic love as a necessary prerequisite to establishing a marital relationship

The Association between Romantic Love and Marriage

Published by New Generation Publishing in 2021

First Edition

ISBN 978-1-80369-068-1

www.newgeneration-publishing.com

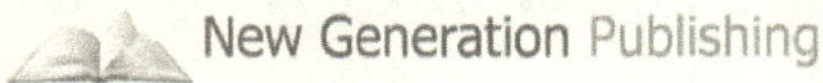
New Generation Publishing

CONTENT

DEDICATION

I would like to dedicate this book to all men and women in the world who are single, married, planning to get married, those in any relationships, planning to go in relationships and the divorced.

You must know you are all created in God's image and you are handsome, beautiful, wonderfully made, amazing, dedicated, respectable, sensitive, knowledgeable, wise, patient, favoured, principled and with great characters. Love is God. Love is an intense feeling of deep affection. For everything we do in life is love. We must become a living model and live with a set standard as well as enjoy your relationships that pleases God. Additionally, this book will also help andguide the unmarried singles who desire to get a successful marriage that God originally intended. This book will also help all married couples whose interest and desire is to have a successful marriage as well as improve it. May the Lord our God give you favour and grace to apply His love and marriage principles in your relationships. Always remember the golden marriage and relationship principle in the bible that is written in proverbs 24:3-4. It states that By wisdom a house is built and through understanding it is established; through knowledge its rooms are filled with rare and beautiful treasures.

PREFACE

The greatest disappointment and yet the utmost joy is found in love and relationships. Love is God. Love is an intense feeling of deep affection. Phileo is love on love of casual friendships, the affection we have for someone we are familiar with. Many people claim to love each other but hope they understand the true meaning of love. Storge describes the tender affection of parents towards their children and that of children towards their parents. This is so important for parent to children relationship. Eross embraces sexual longing, craving, and desire with no respect for scarcity, sensual ecstasy that leaves moderation and proportion far behind. Sex is not love, not spiritual, one hundred percent physical and chemical, appetite, procreation, recreation, release, communication but sexual fulfilment and happiness in marriage is dependent on open loving, accepting and affirming environment that desires each other. This is unfortunately common today in this so called modernity. Agape refers to divine love, the love God has for His people as well as the love His people give back to Him. Agape is unconditional, self-giving, oneness, a Person, others conscious, self- initiating, responsibility, proactive, choice and never changes. Agape is patient, kind, does not envy, does not boast, is not rude, not self-seeking, not easily angered, keeps no record of wrongs, protects, preserves and never fails. Marriage is still a good idea because it is God's idea. Marriage is a foundation institutional that predates all others. Procreation is not the primary purpose of marriage. Marriage as God designed is like precious gem just like monogamous birds that stay committed to each other for life. Godly marriage develops overtime and grows stronger under pressure even in any form of crisis or during turmoil. A Godly relationship or marriage is a union that creates oneness. This means that marriage must remain a steady, unchanging institution entered into by two people who are constantly changing as they grow and mature. The institution of marriage is more important than our personal feeling but not more important than singleness. Commitment to marriage is more important than commitment to a person. Always remember that God will only join what He allows. What God has joined no man, society and government must separate. Lastly a successful marriage hinges on knowledge, wisdom and understanding as well as application of God's principles. God is the author of love and marriage. May God have mercy and give grace to who are going through relationship challenges in this pandemic in Jesus name.

INTRODUCTION

INTRODUCTION OF LOVE

Love in the spiritual realm is a place of absolute peace, motionless, timeless, completely at rest and that has a positive impact on one's emotional, physical and spiritual fulfilment. In fact this is known as agape. Agape is divine love, the love Almighty God has a purpose for His people and return it back to Him. Agape love is unconditional love, a Person, self-giving, oneness, initiating, and takes responsibility, proactive, a choice, unchangeable and conscious of others. In the physical realm love can be defined as the Eros. This embraces sexual longing, craving and desire with no respect for holiness; sensual state that leaves moderation and proportional far behind. This kind of love is often lead by physical attraction and emotions also can result into marriage that brings human joy, fear, intimacy and pain as the most common perspective of this drama.

Another kind of love is Phileo. This kind of love is associated with casual friendship, affection one has for someone he or she is familiar with. It also describes the tender affection of parents towards their children and that of children towards their parents. On the other hand another kind of love is that which is guided by emotions. Emotional love is guided and lead by feelings of love release several chemical compounds and hormones that are in charge of producing the experimentation of a series of determined emotions. In this way, love releases mainly dopamine, serotonin and oxytocin hormones. This kind of love changes with changes of chemical compounds or hormones over time.

Dopamine and serotonin are chemical messengers, or neurotransmitters, that help regulate many bodily functions. They have roles in sleep and memory, as well as metabolism and emotional well-being. People sometimes refer to dopamine and serotonin as the "happy hormones" due to the roles they play in regulating mood and emotion. They are also involved in several mental health conditions, including low mood and depression. Dopamine and serotonin are involved in similar bodily processes, but they operate differently. Imbalances of these chemicals can cause different medical conditions that require different treatments.

DIFFENT KINDS OF LOVE IN THE SPIRITUAL REALM

What is the meaning of agape love?

Agape, and its verb form agape, is one of the several Greek words for love. The Bible also mentions phileo, or brotherly love, and refers to eros, erotic love. The Greeks also spoke of storage, which is a love between family members.

Agape love is a little different. It is not a feeling; it's a motivation for action that we are free to choose or reject. Agape is a sacrificial love that voluntarily suffers inconvenience, discomfort, and even death for the benefit of another without expecting anything in return. We are called to agape love through Christ's example: "Therefore be imitators of God, as beloved children. And walk in love, as Christ loved us and gave himself up for us, a fragrant offering and sacrifice to God" (Ephesians 5:1-2).

We are to agape God (Matthew 22:37), our neighbour (Matthew 22:39), and even our enemies (Matthew 5:43-46). We are not to agape money (Matthew 6:24), darkness (John 3:19), or men's approval (John 12:43).

The New Testament has over two-hundred references to agape love. Here are a few. Matthew 24:12: With increased lawlessness in the end times, concern and caring for others will fade.

➤ Luke 11:42: The legalism of the Pharisees, even their sacrifices, did not reflect a love of God.

➤ John 13:35: The Christian life is characterized by sacrificial agape love.

➤ John 15:9-10; Romans 13:10: When we agape love God, we show it by obeying His commandments because His commandments teach us how to love others.

➤ John 15:13: The greatest demonstration of love anyone can give is to die for his friends.

➤ John 17:26; Romans 5:5; Galatians 5:22: Agape love comes from God, not our own effort.

➤ Romans 5:8; Revelation 1:5: It was agape love that caused Jesus to sacrifice Himself for us.

➤ Romans 14:15; 1 Corinthians 8:1: It is not loving to lead another into sin.

➤ Colossians 3:19: Men are called to show agape love to their wives.

➤ James 1:12; 2:5: Love of God will result in rewards in heaven.

➤ 2 Peter 2:15; 1 John 2:15: It is possible to sacrificially love something that is not godly.

Although 1 Corinthians 13 is known as the chapter on

love, there is no book that speaks more about agape than 1 John. Two important themes come out of 1 John. The first is that it is inconsistent and false to claim we agape love God while not agape loving other believers. We cannot love God without loving brothers and sisters who also love Him. The second is that it is inconsistent and false to claim we agape love God if we don't obey Him. It is impossible to love God while ignoring what He says. The two are inextricably connected, as Galatians 5:14 says: "For the whole law is fulfilled in one word: 'You shall love your neighbour as yourself.'"

What is the meaning of phileo love?

The Greek language has terms for four kinds of love. These terms are phileo, agape, storage, and eros. The two latter Greek terms for love are not mentioned in the Bible, although we do see them expressed in certain stories. To better understand phileo love, it must be defined as one part of these four terms.

Storage is affectionate love. This love exists naturally between family members and friends, such as the warm, unforced love shown between spouses, or between a parent and a child. Storage love is displayed in many stories in the Bible, such as in the stories of Noah, Jacob, and Mary, Martha, and Lazarus.

Eros is sexual or passionate love. Song of Solomon

paints the best example of this love. God created this love, just as He created all the other sides of love, and it is important within a marriage relationship. But the Bible also warns against eros outside of the husband and wife marital relationship (1 Corinthians 6:18; 1 Thessalonians 4:3).

Agape love is sacrificial love. This is the most noble and powerful type of lovebecause it is an act of the will. Christ showed us agape love when he died on the cross, sacrificing Himself so that we can know eternal life and salvation.

Phileo love is brotherly love. This type of love is most often shown within close friendships. This is a generous and affectionate love that seeks to make the other person happy with no expectation for the acts of kindness to be returned. David and Jonathan are one of the Bible's best examples of phileo love within a friendship. First Samuel 18:1–3 describes their friendship and says, in part, that "… the soul of Jonathan was knit to the soul of David, and Jonathan loved him as his own soul. … Then Jonathan made a covenant with David, because he loved him as his own soul."

Phileo love is shown toward people we feel warm and affectionate to. This means that we do not show our enemies phileo love because we do not feel warm and affectionate toward them. However, God does call us to show agape love toward those individuals we dislike and clash with (Luke 6:28; Matthew 5:44). As we grow closer to God and experience more of His compassion, we may even experience phileo love toward people we are beginning to understand better.

WHAT IS EROS LOVE?

Unlike English, in which the word *love* means many different things, Ancient Greek had four words to describe the range of meaning that our word *love* conveys. The first word is *eros*, from which we get the English word *erotic*. *Eros* was the word often used to express sexual love or the feelings of arousal that are shared between people who are physically attracted to one another. The word was also used as the name of the Greek god of love, Eros (the Romans called him "Cupid"). By New Testament times, this word had become so debased by the culture that it is not used even once in the entire New Testament.

The second Greek word for "love" was storage, which referred to natural, familial love. *Storage* (a word not found in the Bible) referred to the type of love shown by a parent for a child. The third Greek word for "love" was *philia*, which forms part of the words *philosophy* ("love of wisdom") and *philanthropy* ("love of fellow man"). This word speaks of the warm affection shared between friends.

Whereas *eros* is more closely associated with the libido, *philia* is associated with the heart (metaphorically speaking). We feel love for our friends and family, obviously not in an erotic sense, but in the sense of being kind and affectionate. However, *philia* is not felt between people who are at enmity with one another. We can feel *philia* toward friends and family, but not toward people whom we dislike or hate.

Different from all of these is the fourth Greek word for "love," *agape*, typically defined as the "self-sacrificing love." This is the love that moves people into action and looks out for the well-being of others, no matter the personal cost. Biblically speaking, *agape* is the love God showed to His people in sending His Son, Jesus, to die for their sins. It is the love that focuses on the will, not the emotions, experience, or libido. This is the love that Jesus commands His disciples to show toward their enemies (Luke 6:35). *Eros* and *philia* are not expressed to people who hate us and wish us ill; *agape* is. In Romans 5:8, Paul tells us that God's love for His people was made manifest in that "while we were still sinners [i.e., enemies], Christ died for us."

So, moving from the base to the pure, we have *eros*, *storage*, *philia*, and *agape*. This is not to denigrate *eros* as sinful or impure. Sexual love is not inherently unclean or evil. Rather, it is the gift of God to married couples to express their love for one another, strengthen the bond between them, and ensure the survival of the human race. The Bible devotes one whole book to the blessings of erotic, or sexual, love—Song of Solomon. The love between a husband and a wife should be, among other things, an erotic love. However, a long-term relationship based solely on *eros* is doomed to failure. The "thrill" of sexual love wears off quickly unless there are some *philia* and *agape* to go along with it.

Even though there is nothing inherently sinful with erotic

love, it is in this sphere that our sinful nature is easily made manifest because *eros* focuses primarily on sensuality and self. *Storage, philia,* and *agape* focus on relationship and others. Consider what the apostle Paul tells the Colossian church: "Put to death therefore what is earthly in you: sexual immorality, impurity, passion, evil desire, and covetousness, which is idolatry" (Colossians 3:5). The Greek word for "sexual immorality" is *porneia* (the root of our word *pornography*). This essentially covers the gamut of sexual sin (adultery, fornication, homosexuality, bestiality, etc.).

When shared between husband and wife, erotic love can be a wonderful thing, but because of our fallen sin nature, expressions of *eros* too often become *porneia*. In dealing with *eros*, human beings tend to go to extremes, becoming either ascetics or hedonists. The ascetic completely eschews sensual or sexual love. The hedonist sees unrestrained sexual passion and all forms of sensuality as perfectly natural and to be indulged. The biblical view is a balance between these two sinful extremes. Within the bond of heterosexual marriage, God celebrates the beauty of sexual love: "Let my lover come into his garden and taste its choice fruits. I have come into my garden, my sister, my bride; I have gathered my myrrh with my spice. I have eaten my honeycomb and my honey; I have drunk my wine and my milk. Eat, O friends, and drink; drink your fill, O lovers" (Song of Solomon 4:16—5:1). Outside of biblical marriage, *eros* becomes distorted and sinful.

WHAT ARE THE FIVE LOVE LANGUAGES?

Gary Chapman's book The Five Love Languages: The Secret to Love That Lasts (Northfield Publishing, 2015) describes five primary ways people receive and express love. It is on the New York Times best-sellers list, and has been since 2007. The first 5 Love Languages ® book was published in 1992. New editions were published in 1995, 2004, 2010, and 2015. Several companion books, such as The Five Love Languages of Teenagers and The Five Love Languages Singles Edition, have since been published. There are also conferences and a website with further resources. What are these five love languages that have been helpful for so many to understand?

According to Chapman, every person can both receive and express love in multiple ways. However, typically there is one primary method that makes a person most easily feel loved. Chapman has identified five of the main ways people feel loved and express their love to others—the five love languages. He explains that understanding one another's love languages helps us to better express love to and receive love from one another. This, of course, has positive effects on our relationships. Those love languages are: Words of Affirmation, Quality Time, Gifts, Acts of Service, and Physical Touch.

Words of Affirmation are words that affirm other people, and in so doing express love to them. This love language uses spoken and written encouragement, compliments, and appreciation to show the other person how much they are loved. It might be something as simple as saying "I'm proud of you", or it could be something as thought out as a letter describing positive attributes of the other person and the many ways for which you are grateful for him or her. People whose primary love language is Words of Affirmation will feel built up and well-cared for when they hear these kinds of words expressed to them or about them. Paul called the Ephesians to, "Let no corrupting talk come out of your mouths, but only such as is good for building up, as fits the occasion, that it may give grace to those who hear" (Ephesians 4:29). Heeding this call helps ensure that those whose primary love language is Words of Affirmation will feel well-loved.

Quality Time is the act of giving the other person your undivided attention. It means spending time focused on togetherness, not just physical proximity to one another. It includes conversing in sympathetic dialogue, sharing experiences together, and purposely doing something the other person enjoys. Expressing your love with your attention and time is what makes people feel loved who have Quality Time as their primary love language. Perhaps this love language is why God commanded that, "When a man is newly married, he shall not go out with the army or be liable for any other public duty. He shall be free at home one year to be happy with his wife whom he has taken" (Deuteronomy 24:5). A year of time together would certainly help build a strong marriage, although ten minutes of your undivided attention each day can speak volumes to those who receive love best in this way.

For those whose primary love language is Gifts, receiving any gift, no matter how small, will express love to them. A gift is a physical symbol of that person's thought toward their loved one. Handmade gifts or free giveaways brought home to the loved one often carry as much meaning as expensive or more elaborate gifts to those with this primary love language because those objects are visual tokens of your caring attitude toward them. Interestingly, while those whose love language is Quality Time desire your attention and not your mere proximity, those whose love language is Gifts often see your physical presence as a gift. Jesus referenced the act of gift giving as a way in which parents naturally express love to their children and how gift giving reflects one characteristic of God the Father. He said, "If you then, who are evil, know how to give good gifts to your children, how much more will your Father who is in heaven give good things to those who ask him!" (Matthew 7:11).

Acts of Service are deeds that help or serve the other person. Giving another person you're planning, time, effort, and energy to serve them can be a powerful expression of love. There are many chores that have to be done in order to run an orderly life. Freely choosing to do one of these helpful deeds with a positive attitude expresses love in a meaningful way to those for whom

Acts of Service is their primary love language. Jesus called His followers to serve one another, pointing out that service is one way He expressed His love for the world. He said, "even as the Son of Man came not to be served but to serve, and to give his life as a ransom for many" (Matthew 20:28).

Physical Touch is the fifth love language. For those whose primary love language is touch, they feel most loved when their bodies are handled in caring ways. These ways include simple actions like holding hands, sitting close together, a gentle back rub, or a tight squeeze. Of course, more involved ways of touching are welcome in marriage like intimate massage and sexual love making. For them, to touch their body is to touch their inner being. It means they are seen, noticed, and cared for. Parents in the Bible understood the importance of physical touch when they brought their children to Jesus not just to hear His teaching, but "that he might lay his hands on them and pray" (Matthew 19:13). And of course, Jesus approved by responding, "Let the little children come to me" (Matthew 19:14). Physical touch is perhaps the love language most likely to be misinterpreted in modern culture. So if you are a person who expresses love through touch, it would be wise to ensure that your friends are similarly comfortable with your expressions of love.

Determining the way in which you most easily experience love and the way in which those around you best receive love can strengthen your relationships. As followers of Christ, we are called to use all of these methods to love one another and those around us. Gary Chapman's book The Five Love Languages contains timeless wisdom and practical help to support living out the command to "Love your neighbour as yourself" (Leviticus 19:18; see also James 2:8; John 13:34– 35).

WHAT DOES THE BIBLE SAY ABOUT FALLING IN LOVE?

Most everybody desires to fall in love. As humans we share an innate longing to experience a special soul-level connection with someone. The world has tried to explain this phenomenon for centuries. Fairy tales depict a destined love at first sight, old married couples reminisce on years of friendship, and scientists study the role of pheromones in physical attraction. The Bible tells us that humans were made for relationship with one another and relationship with God (Genesis 2:18; Matthew 22:36–40). Not everyone is designed for a marriage relationship, but the longing to be loved and to love is part of what it is to be human. For many people, marriage is a key part of this love. The Bible tells us marriage is an image of Christ's relationship with the Church (Ephesians 5:22–33). In the Western world, marriage is often preceded by falling in love.

The Bible does not talk specifically about falling in love, but it does have a lot to say about love. Here it is important to distinguish between different types of love. The Greek, the original language in which the New Testament was written, had four different terms for love: agape (self-sacrificial love), phileo (brotherly love or love between friends), storage (familial or affectionate love), and eros (sexual or passionate love). While our English word love covers a broad spectrum of types of love, we understand that there is a big difference between loving pizza, loving one's parents, and loving one's spouse. Falling in love is often a mixture of different types of love. Sometimes it is more about lusting after a person or an emotional high (perhaps more like eros love). Other times falling in love is a genuine connection and companionship, a sense of knowing and being known, and a desire to walk through life with one another. It develops into a true, committed, lifelong decision to love the other regardless what may come.

The Bible describes true love as selfless, kind, forgiving, unifying, patient, healing, and sacrificial (for example, see 1 Corinthians 13; Colossians 3:12 –14). We are also told that "God is love" (1 John 4:16). When people love one another, it is a choice and a commitment. It is an act of service someone does in order to improve the condition of someone else. It is intentional and not dependent on how someone is feeling or what circumstances they are in. Jesus loved everyone. He loved both those who followed Him and those who condemned Him to the cross.

The world often equates falling in love with a surge of romantic emotions propelled by hormones. It is dependent upon physical attraction, happy circumstances, and strong feelings. Under this definition of love, it is easy to fall out of love when things get difficult or when our feelings change. With the worldly way of thinking, it is easy to excuse divorce, adultery, and casual sex because of how we feel. Physical attraction and happy romantic emotions are not wrong in and of themselves; they can be a wonderful expression of love. However, the foundation of love must be rooted in God. Otherwise these feelings can be hijacked by sinful motives such as lust and infatuation. It is only with God that we can commit to selflessly serve another person regardless of how we are feeling or what is happening around us.

The Song of Solomon gives us the best example in the Bible of romantic love. King Solomon and his wife express all the intense emotions of being in love, yet it is evident that this is an unconditional love founded upon commitment. "Set me as a seal upon your heart, as a seal upon your arm, for love is strong as death, jealousy is fierce as the grave. Its flashes are flashes of fire, the very flame of the Lord. Many waters cannot quench love, neither can floods drown it. If a man offered for love all the wealth of his house, it would be utterly despised" (Song of Solomon 8:6–7).

So instead of waiting to fall in love with that perfect soulmate, choose to live a life motivated by true love found only in God. Then when you do meet someone special and fall in love it won't be by chance, it will be intentional. Instead of dreading the end of the honeymoon stage, you can look forward to cultivating a deeper love than you ever imagined possible.

DOES THE BIBLE TALK ABOUT DATING / COURTING?

The words "dating" or "courting" do not appear in the Bible, yet God's Word does have wisdom to offer about these relationships before marriage.

The ultimate goal of biblical dating is to discover and confirm a marriage partner. A Christian who dates to get to know someone with marriage in mind should be asking several questions.

First, is this person a Christian (John 3:3–8)? The Bible tells us not to enter into partnerships with those who are not fellow believers (2 Corinthians 6:14–15). A lifelong spouse is the ultimate partner.

Also, does this person desire to grow in their relationship with Jesus, becoming more like Him (Philippians 2:1–11; Romans 12:1–2; John 15:1-17)? Does this person put their relationship with God as a priority over all others, even you (Matthew 10:37)? Are they removing idols from their life (Galatians 5:20; Colossians 3:5)?

Does the person you want to date have a commitment to abstain from sex until marriage (1 Corinthians 6:9, 18; 2 Timothy 2:22)? Though many in society engage in so-called casual sex or even serial monogamy in committed dating, there is no place in biblical dating or courtship for sex. Christians are called to sexual purity in both actions and thought. In a committed marriage between husband and wife, sex is a beautiful and meaningful gift. Save this gift for marriage.

Also ask yourself some questions. Does this person help or hinder your walk with Christ? Are you making sure not to idolize this person or your relationship, or even the goal of marriage? Are you able to remain sexually pure with this person? Do you feel comfortable to be yourself with this person? Are you being honest in the relationship? Are you feeling challenged to grow in this relationship?

Dating is a time when people get to know one another on a deeper level. We discover things about each other's personality, likes and dislikes, hopes and dreams by spending time together. A good marriage partner will exhibit character traits of God such as generosity, forgiveness, grace, mercy, love, selflessness, patience, and righteousness. They will also help us to exhibit these traits.

God designed marriage between one man and one woman to become one, to be married for a lifetime, and to honour Him (Genesis 2:24; Matthew 19:5). Spouses should encourage one another in their walks with the Lord and help each other become more godly. A good marriage involves both spouses giving selflessly of their love to one another. It is about knowing and being known, being authentic with one another and partnering in life together with God's love. A dating relationship is one in which you get to know the other person and determine if marriage would be a good fit.

Consider your motives for dating and compare them to what God desires for relationships and marriage. Seek His wisdom (James 1:5) and proceed with purity and joy. Whether a dating relationship turns into a marriage or not, it is an opportunity to get to know another person, grow in your relationship with Christ, and to exhibit God's love.

CAN YOU LOVE A PERSON BUT NOT LIKE THEM?

Jesus tells His disciples, and by extension all of His followers, to love each other (John 13:34), their neighbours (Luke 10:25–37), their enemies (Luke 6:27–28)— in essence, everyone. But He does not say that we must like everyone or be friends with everyone.

The Greek word for love in each of the passages mentioned above is agape, or agape love. Agape love is a selfless, often sacrificial, love wherein the object of love is the most important person in the exchange. It is a love that looks to the best interests of others and acts to meet those interests. Agape love does not necessarily require affection as it is not primarily about the emotions of those involved.

Jesus sets the example for us with His sacrificial love. Romans 5:8 says, "but God shows his love for us in that while we were still sinners, Christ died for us." First John

4:19 says, "We love because he first loved us." Our response to God's undeserved love for us is to love others—deservingly or not.

We see in Jesus' life demonstration of love for what would be considered "undesirables." He called lowly fishermen and hated tax collectors as disciples; interacted with the despised Samaritans; and showed "sinners," Romans, women, children, and even the corrupt religious leaders of the day care, patience, forgiveness, and love. Whether to the outcasts of society or the people antagonist toward Him, Jesus demonstrated true love to others. This was not always a comfortable or affectionate love, but was always truthful and a demonstration of God's grace.

It will take the power of the Holy Spirit at work in us to love those we don't like. Often in seeking to love others in a way that is for their benefit, we find ourselves disliking them less. It is difficult to both despise someone emotionally and love them in deed at the same time. But there may also be people who we simply dislike, no matter what we do, whom we are still called upon to love.

When we decide to view each person as a creation of God made in His image, as someone He loves and for whom Jesus willingly died on the cross so that God could reconcile people to Himself (2 Corinthians 5:19–21), it becomes easier to love with God's love. The more we have God's perspective, the less it will matter whether we like a person or not.

One important caution: Love is not the same thing as trust. Some people cannot be trusted and we are not called, usually, to put ourselves in physical or emotional danger in order to love someone. Jesus removed Himself from the crowds for His own protection at times because He knew their hearts (John 5:13; 6:15). We, too, can be wise in the specific actions we are called to take in love. Ask God for wisdom and discernment (James 1:5).

As we become more aware of God's deep love for us and grow in His truth and our love for Him, we are increasingly able to love others with godly love. The more we know God and allow Him to work in us, the more His love will flow through us, regardless of affection (Galatians 5:22–23).

WHAT DOES THE BIBLE SAY ABOUT ENGAGEMENT?

A Christian engagement should reflect the fact that marriage is a God-created, God-ordained institution meant to support individuals in a loving relationship and strengthen them to serve God and others. Scripture is specific that the couple should remove themselves from their childhood families and be devoted to one another (Mark 10:7-9). The Bible also says that disloyalty to the marriage commitment is akin to rejecting God.

The Bible does not dictate how Christians should spend their engagement, although there are allusions to how engagements worked in Bible times. Usually marriages were arranged to the benefit of the families and their patriarchs—not the feelings of the individuals involved. The groom would approach the bride's father and set terms, including the dowry which was supposed to be a nest egg for the woman if her husband should die or divorce her without giving her a child. The groom would return to his father's house and build a room for the future couple. Sometime later, he would go get his bride and bring her to the prepared space. They would have the marriage ceremony, the families would celebrate, and the bride would become a member of the groom's family.

A modern take on a godly relationship would look a little different, but it would still have three similar stages. The first would be two individuals recognizing each other as potential marriage partners, either through friendship or dating. This is the time for big issues to come to light including faith (2 Corinthians 6:14-15), family obligations, personal challenges, and even struggles with sin. Both individuals need to know enough to be able to make an informed decision as to whether they can be compatible as a couple. And they need to take the time to ask God if this is the right person (Proverbs 3:5-6).

The second stage, engagement, is an important time for Christians. Once a couple has either resolved or agreed to accept the big issues in each other's lives, they can make the commitment to work toward marriage. Like the Israelite groom who builds a living space for his bride-to-be, engaged Christian couples should spend this time preparing. The emphasis shouldn't be on the ceremony, which may only last a few minutes, but on practical and relational matters that will ensure the marriage is strong. A good premarital counsellor will cover finances, housing, expectations of roles, and how childhood families create paradigms that can be completely foreign to the other partner. In addition, men need to learn how to love sacrificially (Ephesians 5:25), and women need to learn to respect their man (Ephesians 5:33).

The third step, marriage, is much bigger than the feelings of two people in one moment. If done properly and thoroughly, the skills learned during the engagement period should serve the couple throughout their marriage. This means a Christian engagement is not a time to try things out to see if they work. It is not a chance for the couple to make sure they're sexually compatible; it's a time to develop communication skills that can be the basis for a healthy sexual relationship (1 Corinthians 7:3-5). It's not a time to determine if a couple can live together without driving each other nuts; it's a time to learn how to love sacrificially (Philippians 2:3). Resolution skills, love, and communication are surer signs of a lasting marriage than convenient personal compatibility at a particular stage in life.

In general, a Christian engagement should lead to marriage. It is a commitment to another person, and such commitments should be honoured. But it is not a sin to break off the engagement if events occur or issues come to light that cause the couple to re-evaluate the appropriateness of their match. Unlike in Bible times, breaking off an engagement is not divorce. But modern engagements should carry a similar weight as the two learn how to be one. If done right, the few months or years of engagement will equip the couple for many years of good life together.

INTRODUCTION OF MARRIAGE

Different definitions of marriage
Different sociologist have tried to define it.
They differ from each other.

- ➤ According to sociology journal of cultures, "Marriage is a physical, legal and moral union between man and woman in complete community life for the establishment of a family."

- ➤ According to Malinowski, "Marriage is a contract for the production and maintenance of children."

- ➤ Edward Westermark in his famous book 'History of human marriage' defined, "Marriage is a relation of one or more men to one or more women which is recognized by customs or law and involves certain rights and duties both in case of parties entering into the union and in the case of children born of it."

➢ According to H.M. Johnson, "Marriage is a stable relationship in which a man and a woman are socially permitted without loss of standing in community to have children."

➢ According to Lowie, "Marriage is a relatively permanent bond between permissible mates."

➢ According to Horton and Hunt, "Marriage is the approved social pattern whereby two or more persons establish a family."

➢ According to Hoebel, "The complexes of social norms that define and Control the relations of a mated pair to each other their kinsmen, their offspring and their society at large."

➢ Thus from the above analysis it is

concluded that marriage is both a biological, psychological, cultural and social affair. Marriage is a special type of relationship between permissible mates involving certain rights and obligations. This means "Marriage consists of the rules and regulations which define the rights, duties and privileges of husband and wife with respect to each other."

CHARACTERISTICS OF MARRIAGE:

Marriage may have the following characteristics.

➢ Marriage is a universal social institution. It is found in almost all societies and at all stages of development.

➢ Marriage is a permanent bond between husband and wife. It is designed to fulfil the social, psychological, biological and religious aims.

➢ Marriage is a specific relationship between two individuals of opposite sex and based on mutual rights and obligations. Relationship is enduring.

- Marriage requires social approval. The relationship between men and women must have social approval. Without which marriage is not valid.

- Marriage establishes family. Family helps in providing facilities for the procreation and upbringing of children.

- Marriage creates mutual obligations between husband and wife. The couple fulfil their mutual obligations on the basis of customs or rules.

- Marriage is always associated with some civil and religious ceremony. This social and religious ceremony provides validity to marriage. Though modern marriage performed in courts still it requires certain religious or customary practices.

- Marriage regulates sex relationship according to prescribed customs and laws.

- Marriage has certain symbols like ring, vermillion, special cloths, special sign before the house etc.

TYPES OF MARRIAGE:

➤ As a universal social institution marriage is found to exist in all societies and at all stages of development. Types or forms of marriage varies from society to society. Types or forms of marriage in different communities, societies and cultural groups differ according to their customs, practices and systems of thought. In some societies marriage is a religious sacrament whereas in others it is a social contract. However, there are several types of marriage which is classified on different basis.

➤ On the basis of number of mates:

➤ On the basis of number of mates marriage may be classified into three types such as Monogamy, Polygamy and Endogamy or group marriage. This can be known from the following diagram.

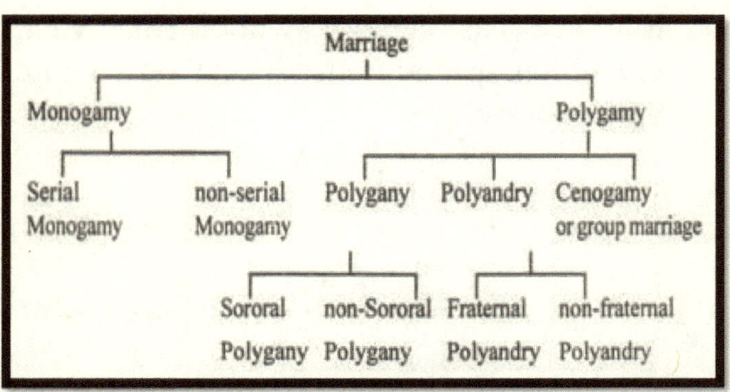

Monogamy:

Monogamy is an ideal, widespread and rational type of marriage. It is found in all civilized societies. Monogamy refers to a marriage of one man with one woman at a time. This type of marriage is normally unbreakable in nature. It continue till death. Today the principle of monogamy i.e. one husband and one wife is practised and emphasised throughout the world. Monogamy is of two types such as serial Monogamy and non-serial Monogamy.

Serial Monogamy:

In serial Monogamous marriage the possibility of remarriage exists in case of divorce or death. In spite of his remarriage he remains to be monogamous.

Non-serial Monogamy:

In case of non-serial monogamy the question of remarriage does not arise by either of the couple. Here a spouse has the same single spouse throughout his life. However, Monogamy is an ideal or best form of marriage because of its different advantages which are as follows:

> - It is suitable for all society and for all levels of people.

> - It provide better sex satisfaction to both husband and wife.

> - It promotes better understanding between the spouse.

> It minimizes jealousy, hatred and quarrels in the family.

> It upholds gender equality and provides equal status to men and women.

> It provides stable sex-life and stable family life.

Children are taken proper care by parents.

It facilitates easy rules of inheritance and succession. Because of the above advantages Monogamy is considered as the best form of marriage and is practiced everywhere. The only disadvantages of Monogamy is divorce which is resulted due to the monogamous boredom.

Polygamy:

Polygamy is a type of marriage in which there is plurality of partners. It allows a man to marry more than one woman or a woman to marry more than one man at a time. Polygamy is of three types such as polygamy, polyandry and endogamy or group marriage.

Polygamy:

Polygamy is a type of marriage in which a man marries more than one wife at a time. In this type of marriage each wife has her separate household and the husband visits them in turn. It was a preferred form of marriage in ancient Indian society. But now it was not in practice among majority of population. But it is now found among few tribes such as Naga, Gond and Baiga. Economic and political cause was mainly responsible for polygamy. Besides man's taste for variety, enforced celibacy, Barrenness of women more women population etc. are some of the cause of polygamy. Polygamy is further divided into two types such as sororal polygyny and non- sororal polygyny.

Sorroral Polygamy:

Sorroral polygamy is often called as surrogate. The term surrogate comes from the Latin word 'sorer' which means sister. Accordingly it refers to a marriage practice in which a man marries the sisters of his wife at a time or after the death of his wife.

Non-sororal Polygamy:

It is just opposite of the sororal polygamy, when a man marries several women at a time who are not necessarily sister to each other it is known as non-sororal polygamy.

Polyandry:

Polyandry is a very rare type of marriage in present day. In this type of marriage a woman marries several men at a time. In the words of K.M. Kapadia, "Polyandry is a form of union in which a woman has more than one husband at a time or inwhich brothers share a wife or wives in common. At present it is found among some of the tribes like toda, khasi and nayars. Polyandry is divided into two types such as fraternal polyandry and non-fraternal polyandry.

Fraternal Polyandry:

When several brothers share a common wife it is called as fraternal polyandry. Draupadi's marriage to Pandabs is fine example of fraternal polyandry. The determination of father is associated with some rituals. At present time this type of marriage is practised by some tribes like toda and khasi.

Non-fraternal Polyandry:

It is just opposite of fraternal polyandry. In this type of marriage husbands of a woman is not necessarily brother to each other. This type of marriage is found among the Nayars of Kerala, Wife goes to spend some time with each of her husband. So long as a woman lives with one of her husbands, the others have no claim on her. This mainly happens due to scarcity of women.

Endogamy or Group Marriage:

Endogamy is otherwise known as group marriage. In this type of marriage a group of men marry a group of women at a time. Every woman is the wife of every man belonging to the particular groups. Sociologist, like Dr. Rivers call it as a kind of sexual communism. This type of marriage is found among some tribes of New Guinea and Africa,

On the basis of choice of mate or on the basis of rules of mate selection:

Marriage may be divided into two types i.e. endogamous and exogamous marriages on the basis of choice of mate or on the basis of the rules of choice of mate. Endogamy is divided into four sub types such as caste, sub-caste, varna and tribal endogamy. Similarly exogamous marriage may be divided into four sub-types such as Gotra, Pravar, Sapinda and village exogamy. All this can be presented in the following diagram.

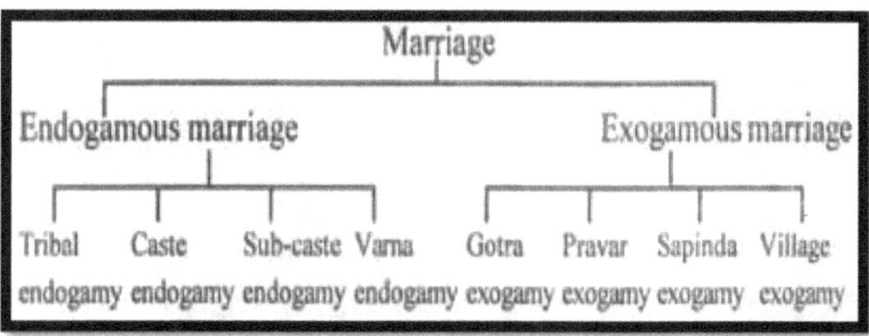

Endogamy or endogamous marriage:

Endogamy or endogamous marriage refers to the marriage within one's own group such as within one's own caste, sub-caste, varna and tribe. In other words there are several types of endogamous marriage such as caste endogamy, sub- caste endogamy, varna endogamy and tribal endogamy.

Caste endogamy:

Caste endogamy is a type of endogamous marriage in which marriage takes place within one's own caste. In a caste based society endogamy is strictly followed. Members of each caste marry within its own caste group.

Sub-caste endogamy:

It is another type of endogamous marriage. In a caste based society each caste is divided into many sub-castes. Like caste each sub-caste is also an endogamous unit. In sub-caste endogamy marriage takes place within one's sub- caste only.

Varna endogamy:

Varna endogamy is another type of endogamous marriage. In the traditional Indian Society we found the existence of four varnas such as Brahmin, Kshatriya, Vaisya and Sudra. In varna endogamy the choice of mate is restricted to one's own varna only.

Tribal endogamy:

Tribe is a territorial group. Tribal endogamy is a type of endogamous married in which the choice of mate is restricted to one's own tribal group. Like caste tribe is also an endogamous unit.

Exogamy or Exogamous marriage:

It is just opposite to the endogamy or endogamous marriage

system. It refers to a system of marriage in which an individual has to marry outside one's own group such as gotra, pravara, sapinda or village. This is a sound marriage system which leads to the creation of healthy and intelligent children. However there are several forms of exogamy such as:

Gotra exogamy:

Gotra refers to clan. Members of a particular gotra or clan supposed to have close blood relation among themselves. Hence according to gotra exogamy one has to marry outside one's own gotra.

Pravara exogamy:

Pravara means siblings. People originating from a common saint are said to belong a particular Pravara. According to Pravara exogamy one has to marry outside one's own pravara. Marriage within pravara is forbidden.

Sapinda exogamy:

Sapinda means-lineage. People belonging to five generations from father side and three or seven generation from mother side are known as sapindas. They believed to belong a particular pinda. Hence according to sapinda exogamy marriage within one's own sapinda is forbidden. They are supposed to marry outside one's own sapnida.

Village exogamy:

According to this principle marriage within one's own village is forbidden each and every society prescribes certain rules relating to marriage. Some societies put several restrictions on marriage among kins whereas some other societies allows marriage between a limited number of kins. Hence in those societies marriage is sanctioned on the basis of preference or priority. Accordingly socially sanctioned marriage among kins is known as preferential marriage. In other words on the basis of preference marriage may be divided into four types such as cross-cousin marriage, parallel cousin marriage, levirate and surrogate.

Cross-cousin marriage:

When marriage takes place between one's mother's brother's daughter/son with father's sister's son/daughter we called it as cross cousin marriage. The marriage of Abhimanyu with Sashikala is an example of this cross-cousin type of marriage. This type of marriage supposed to be practised in some part of Orissa, Rajasthan, and Maharashtra etc. This type of marriage occur to avoid payment of high bride price and to maintain one's family property.

Parallel Cousin marriage:

When marriage takes place between the children of either two sisters or two brothers it is known as parallel cousin marriage. This type of marriage is mostly found among Muslims.

Levirate:

It is otherwise known as 'Devar Vivaha'. When a woman marries her husband's brother after the death of her husband it is known as levirate. This type of marriage is found among some tribes like the Gond, the Munda or the Santal the oran and the Toda etc

Sororate:

It is otherwise known as 'Sali Vivah'. When a man marries his wife's sister after the death of his wife or even when the wife is alive it is called as sororate. This type of marriage is found among some tribes like the Kharia and the Gond.

Anuloma or Pratiloma:

Sociologist have classified marriage into Anuloma or Pratiloma.

Anuloma marriage or Hypergamy:

When a man of higher caste or varna marries a woman of lower caste or varna it is called as Anuloma or Hypergamy marriage. In traditional Indian society hypergamy is known as Anuloma. This was in practice among the nobles in the past. In Bengal it was found in the form of Kulinism.

Pratiloma marriage or Hypogamy:

Pratiloma or hypogamy marriage is just opposite of Anuloma or hypergamy. When a man of lower caste or status marries a woman of higher caste or status it is known as pratiloma or hypogamy marriage. This is not an approved form of marriage. Ancient Hindu law giver a man a lower caste or status marries a woman of higher caste or status it is known as pratiloma or hypogamy marrieage. This is not an approved form of marriage. Ancient Hindu law giver Manu denounced Pratiloma is still it practice among the people.

Marriage is defined differently, and by different entities, based on cultural, religious, and personal factors. A commonly accepted and encompassing definition of marriage is the following: a formal union and social and legal contract between two individuals that unites their lives legally, economically, and emotionally. The contractual marriage agreement usually implies that the couple has legal obligations to each other throughout their lives or until they decide to divorce. Being married also gives legitimacy to sexual relations within the marriage. Traditionally, marriage is often viewed as having a key role in the preservation of morals and civilisation.

Meaning and Types:

Like family, marriage is another important social institution. Marriage and family are two aspects of the same social reality i.e. the bio-psychic and social instincts of man. Marriage is one of the most ancient, important, universal and indispensable social institution which has been in existence since the inception of human civilization.

As an institution marriage is designed to satisfy the biological needs especially the sexual needs of the individual in a legal, customary, culturally defined and socially approved man unilateral descent rule .It also admits men and women to family life and fixes certain rights and duties in respect of children born of their union. As a stable social institution it binds two opposite sexes and allows them to live as husband and wife. It also confers on them social legitimation to have sexual relations and have children. The institutionalized form of sex relations is called marriage. It is closely associated with the institution of family and women to family.

WHAT DOES THE BIBLE TEACH ABOUT MARRIAGE?

Marriage is such a ubiquitous part of every human culture that we tend to forget we didn't create the institution. It is God who created marriage, and He gave some very specific guidance in His word.

What the Bible says about marriage

The Bible uses marriage as a metaphor for the relationship between God and His people. The entire book of Hosea is a story about the unfaithfulness of Israel as allegorized by Hosea's wife—a not-quite reformed prostitute. In Ephesians 5:32, Paul applies the metaphor to the church age. John concurred in Revelation 19:7- 10 where he describes the marriage supper of the Lamb.

Marriage is the ideal situation in which to raise children. Although the Holy Spirit impregnated Mary while she was engaged, God made sure Jesus was born to two loving parents. Several women in the Bible (Genesis 19:30-38; 38:12-26) went to extraordinary lengths to get pregnant, but such measures were not endorsed by Scripture.

Marriage is the only legitimate place for sex (1 Corinthians 7:2-5). The Bible is clear: marriage is the only relationship in which people are to have sex. Marriage takes two people and joins them in purpose. God's mission to rule and subdue and fill the earth is given to all mankind. In marriage, two people work together to fulfil their part of the mission. Perhaps the best example of this is in Aquila and Priscilla. After hearing Apollos preach the limited Gospel he'd heard from John the Baptist, Aquila and Priscilla pulled him aside together and explained the full Gospel of Christ (Acts 18:24-26). It must have worked, as some of the Corinthians revered Apollos more than even Paul (1 Corinthians 3:4-7).

The Bible does not say marriage is mandatory. God does not plan for everyone to marry (1 Corinthians 7:38). Jesus didn't. Jeremiah didn't (Jeremiah 16:2). Likely neither did Paul (1 Corinthians 7:7-8). God has gifted some of His followers to make extreme sacrifices in service to Him without the help or obligation of a spouse.

The purpose of marriage is not to increase a man's power, property, or influence; it's to increase God's. The Israelites were generally very good about getting married and having babies. But although large families helped support their agrarian lifestyle, they did not ensure success. God blessed those who obeyed (Deuteronomy 11:8-9). In the New Testament, God also promises blessings for obedience—heavenly rewards. The role of wives and children is not to increase a man's blessing on earth; wives and children are the blessing (Genesis 2:18; Psalm 127:3-5).

Marriage is not a replacement for a relationship with God. In New Testament times, women had very few rights. They could usually not own property, and their nearest male relative made all the legal decisions. But when Sapphira obeyed her husband in Acts 5 by lying about how much money they had donated to the church, God still judged her as an individual (verse 10). God was not lenient because Sapphira was keeping local custom to obey her husband unquestioningly. Conversely, Abigail was praised when she went behind her foolish husband's back to give proper recompense to David for his protection of their holdings (1 Samuel 25).

The Bible says that marriage is not defined or ordained by mankind (Matthew 19:5-6). The government does not define marriage, although its validation of the marriage may be necessary for civil purposes. Culture does not define marriage. Neither does sentiment. Even the couple in the relationship have no say. God ordained that the man and woman should leave their parents and become one. God joins the two into one. By the same token, mankind does not define the dissolution of marriage, and convenience and regret do not make for divorce. It is the rejection of God's standards, either through sexual sin or disobedience, that creates divorce.

What the Bible says about being married

Finally, the Bible gives some very specific instruction regarding what individuals must do so their marriage can fulfil God's purpose. Each member must deny their natural self-centred inclinations in favour of what is best for the relationship. Husbands must love with self-sacrifice (Ephesians 5:25). Wives should understand that every team has a leader, and God has given that role to the husbands (Ephesians 5:22-23). Wives should also understand that the "helper" of Genesis 2:18 is not an administrative assistant; it is a fierce warrior called to protect and defend. A marriage can't be successful unless both the wife and husband protect each other.

WHAT IS THE PURPOSE OF MARRIAGE?

After God created Adam and placed him in the garden of Eden, He said, "It is not good that the man should be alone; I will make him a helper fit for him" (Genesis 2:18). None of the animals would be a suitable helper; Adam needed someone also made in God's image. So God created Eve, from the rib of Adam, as his helper and companion. Eve was there to help, to comfort, to be as one with Adam. This was the first marriage between man and woman. God created marriage so that no one needed to be alone. God says here that one purpose of marriage is to provide companionship and mutual help and comfort.

Jesus makes reference to Genesis when the Pharisees asked Him about divorce. "He answered, 'Have you not read that he who created them from the beginning made them male and female, and said, "Therefore a man shall leave his father and his mother and hold fast to his wife, and the two shall become one flesh"? So they are no longer two but one flesh. What therefore God has joined together, let not man separate'" (Matthew 19:4-6). Marriage is a union in which two different people—male and female—who both bear the image of God are united and become one. In a marriage, the partners are meant to complement one another, each bringing different things to the relationship and yet becoming as one.

Another purpose of marriage is to produce godly offspring (Malachi 2:15). Marriage brings a sense of stability in the home and one where our children can feel safe, loved, and prosper. Second Corinthians 6:14 is applicable to marriage—the best marriage is that of two believers. God's desire for this holy marriage and offspring is so that we can continue to share the Good News, proclaiming our faith to one another.

The Bible paints a beautiful picture of what marriage should look like, but as sinners, we will stumble. There will be arguments, difficulties, and trials. As believers, if we keep God at the centre of our marriage, He can help us navigate these difficulties in a way that brings Him glory. Marriage will teach us to listen to others, to rid ourselves of selfishness, and to love others, just as God loves us (John 13:34–35). Marriage is fertile ground for God's work of sanctification. If we can come together and discuss our shortcomings and then lift them to God in prayer, He will lead us. Our marriage will thrive.

In a world that is full of sexual temptations, marriage also protects us. Having a husband or wife gives us the security of having a committed sexual relationship that is healthier than the alternative. Any sexual relations or temptations outside of marriage will often to lead to destruction emotionally, physically, mentally, and spiritually.

Marriage is also a picture of Christ and His Church (Ephesians 5:21–33). In part, this is what makes sexual sin such a big issue. God is completely faithful to us, and calls us to be completely faithful both to Him and to our spouse. Marriage is thought to be a holy institution because it was created at the beginning. The image of marriage related to Christ and the church also helps us understand why marriage is distinct and to be honoured.

Proverbs 18:22 says, "He who finds a wife [or husband] finds a good thing and obtains favour from the LORD" (Proverbs 18:22). Indeed, marriage is a gift from God and filled with purpose.

WHAT SHOULD I BE LOOKING FOR IN A WIFE?

The most important attribute a man should look for in a future wife is whether she loves and follows Jesus. Her first priority, and yours, should be God. In the Bible, we are told to marry someone with whom we are equally yoked, meaning another believer (2 Corinthians 6:14). When we marry another Christian, as a couple, our lives' purposes will be aligned.

Many women may profess to be Christians. It is crucial that you choose a woman who has not only accepted Christ as her Saviour, but is also continually maturing in her faith. The Bible provides two key descriptions of the role of a wife in marriage. First, in Genesis, God created Eve as a helper for Adam (Genesis 2:20–24). A godly wife faithfully supports and partners with her husband in serving God. Secondly, in the book of Ephesians, Paul says, "Wives, submit to your own husbands, as to the Lord" (Ephesians 5:22). Wives should respect their husbands and willingly serve and love them. They should acknowledge that God has placed their husband as head of the household so that they might protect, provide for, and love their wives. A godly wife does not submit to her husband out of fear or feelings of inadequacy, but rather out of respect and trust.

Proverbs 31 provides many wonderful descriptions of a God-honouring woman. "An excellent wife who can find? She is far more precious than jewels. The heart of her husband trusts in her, and he will have no lack of gain. She does him good, and not harm, all the days of her life" (Proverbs 31:10–12). You should look for a woman who is trustworthy, hard-working, responsible, caring, and fears the Lord. These are women like Esther, Abigail, and Mary who were brave, wise, and strong, yet demonstrated both respect and love towards God and the men in their lives.

In addition, you should seek a wife who shares similar interests and goals, political and doctrinal beliefs, and moral values. Together you should talk about one another's expectations regarding children, finances, and other issues you'll face as a married couple; it is important to have these conversations before you get married. You should find someone you are romantically and physically attracted to and, more importantly, who helps you to be your best.

You will never find the perfect wife, but you can find a wife who faithfully serves God and will respect and love you faithfully as well.

WHAT SHOULD I BE LOOKING FOR IN A HUSBAND?

When seeking a husband, the most important criteria a woman should look for is if the man loves and follows Jesus; we want a husband who could be said to be a man after God's heart. Although our spouse should have priority among our human relationships, our relationship with God is the most important. The Bible instructs us to only marry someone with whom we are equally yoked (2 Corinthians 6:14). Equally yoked classifies a person as a fellow follower of Christ. It is crucial that we marry another believer so that, as a couple, our lives' purposes and way of life will be aligned.

Not only should a woman look for a Christian man, but a man who continues to mature in his faith after becoming a believer. The Bible provides numerous descriptions of what a godly man looks like. For example, a godly man is strong, humble, and caring (1 Corinthians 16:13; 1 Peter 5:5; Mark 10:43–45). Jesus Himself is the perfect example. The role a husband plays in relation to his wife symbolizes the role Jesus plays in relation to the Church (Ephesians 5:22–33).

As previously stated, the first quality to look for in a prospective husband is that he is a man after God's own heart. After God removed Saul from the throne of Israel, He appointed David and said, "I have found in David the son of Jesse a man after my heart, who will do all my will" (Acts 13:22). God wants men like David, who understand His will, are obedient to Him, and do the work of His kingdom. Another key quality to look for is a man who loves his wife as he loves himself. In Ephesians chapter 5, Paul describes the role of a husband. He states, "Husbands, love your wives, as Christ loved the church and gave himself up for her... In the same way husbands should love their wives as their own bodies. He who loves his wife loves himself" (Ephesians 5:25, 28). A good husband will love his wife sacrificially and unconditionally. He will be willing to do anything, including laying down his life, in order to care for and protect her. In addition, a husband should be a spiritual leader for his family. As the head of the household he is responsible for helping his wife, and any children they might have, to follow God and for taking care of them (1 Corinthians 11:3; Ephesians 6:4; 1 Timothy 5:8).

If a man embodies the qualities listed above, he will be a faithful and God- honouring husband. However, it is also wise to consider some other factors for a future spouse. You should look for someone with similar interests and goals, political and doctrinal beliefs, and moral values. It is recommended to discuss important topics such as children, residence, extended family, and finances before getting married. You want someone who can bring out the best in you by supporting you while also being honest with you. Physical and romantic attraction are also valid and important things to consider. The perfect husband does not exist. However, if you find a man who is committed to serving God and loves you unconditionally, then you will have found a faithful partner to share this life with.

WITH ALL ITS CHALLENGES, WHY EVEN CONSIDER MARRIAGE?

God's structure for marriage, despite what the world may say otherwise, remains the building block of society. The Bible tells us that God sees marriage as the lifelong commitment between one man and one woman in a God-honouring relationship. Hebrews 13:4 says, "Let marriage be held in honour among all..." It is often said that God instituted marriage in the garden of Eden, and He did. The first married couple was Adam and Eve. Marriage has been God's design for family ever since.

Because God designed men and women, He knows that a lifelong commitment provides stabilization, security, and hope within a marriage. That commitment is expressed through vows to both God and the bride and groom in a marriage ceremony.

God says man and woman are created in His image, therefore the most complete reflection of Him on earth is the lifelong bond of a man and woman (Genesis 1:27–31). His initial purpose of marriage between a God-honouring man and woman was to produce more God-honouring men and women. When men and women enter into a God-honouring marriage, they produce a picture of the relationship between Christ and the church (Ephesians 5:22–32).

God knows, and wise people understand, that people change over time. But marriage is about commitment. A husband's and wife's commitment to love one another are crucial to holding a marriage together through those changes, through difficulties and challenges, and through decades of many circumstances.

Marriage is not intended to be a temporary, self-gratifying arrangement. Marriage is primarily to honour God and then to serve your spouse for a lifetime. Through that unselfishness, each spouse will find contentment and joy. A person's role in a marriage is not primarily to be loved, but to love.

Marriage does have many challenges, but it is also a union in which husband and wife can feel fully accepted and safe. It is a relationship that God uses to encourage His people and to display His love for them. It is a place where husband and wife can both experience and give true agape love. It is also a relationship that God uses to sanctify believers. That is not to say that every Christian must marry. Some people should not (1 Corinthians 7). Both marriage and singleness are gifts from God. Christians reflect God in both life situations.

When a person decides to enter into marriage, they do so by faith (2 Corinthians 5:7). With God's help, marriage can be a solid foundation through the storms of life. Also with God's help, marriages can remain strong and even grow in the midst of challenging circumstances, disappointments, changes, anger, mistakes, and even disasters.

WHAT IS SOME ADVICE FOR MAKING MARRIAGE LAST?

When both the husband and wife each, individually, commit themselves to an obedient, close, growing relationship with God, then to a selfless, caring, committed relationship with each other, their marriage can last.

Second Corinthians 6:14–15 says, "Do not be unequally yoked with unbelievers. For what partnership has righteousness with lawlessness? Or what fellowship has light with darkness? What accord has Christ with Belial? Or what portion does a believer share with an unbeliever?" Marrying another Christian goes a long way in making a marriage last. Most importantly, believers are indwelt by the Holy Spirit, so each spouse will have the Holy Spirit's help in making their relationship strong. Believers should also hold to the same biblical values. For example, both should seek to love the other with the agape love of God and be willing and quick to forgive.

The Bible offers married people much advice. Even more, God tells us we can ask Him for wisdom and He will provide it (James 1:5). Studying the Bible together and praying together for your marriage, as well as doing these things alone and with larger groups of believers, are vital to a lasting marriage.

Ephesians 5 tells married people to selflessly serve one another. The husband should follow God and love, honour, and protect his wife (Ephesians 5:25–33) and the wife should follow God and submit to her husband (Ephesians 5:22–24, 33).

Every marriage benefits from spending time together; voicing admiration and love for one another; serving one another; giving gifts (material and immaterial) to one another; showing kindness, forgiveness, affection, and understanding; and liberally demonstrating love in the way the other spouse best receives it (his or her "love language").

God instituted "oneness" in the first marriage, that between Adam and Eve. He said they became "one flesh" (Genesis 2:23–24). This means more than the physical bonding; it includes a oneness of mind and purpose. This type of unity is possible and much enhanced when both people in a marriage take their marriage vows before God seriously.

All couples will experience degrees of trouble and rough going. During these times, it is important to communicate clearly, to avoid manipulation or making threats (for example, using the threat of divorce for shock value), and to commit to finding resolution. Fight for your marriage together. If one spouse "wins" and the other "loses," both have lost. Husband and wife should also be willing to get help from others when needed—for example, a godly older Christian couple, pastor, or Christian marriage counsellor.

Prayer is always essential, and even more important during times of hardship. Pray for your marriage and for your own heart to be malleable to God's guidance. Trust that God will hear and guide. Remain committed to your marriage and willing to work toward healing and restoration. When both spouses are seeking God and willing to humbly serve the other, a marriage can last.

Much of the selflessness God calls us to in marriage can be found in many good, solid, long-lasting marriages. What often sets a marriage of two Christians apart from others, is that both the husband and wife funnel their commitment to each other through their vows and relationship with God.

WHAT ARE BIBLICAL STEPS TO RESTORE A MARRIAGE?

Restoring a marriage is a far more complex and involved issue than can be addressed in a this book. Very likely, there are years of hurt behind every cruel word, and quite possibly a lifetime of differences in personality and upbringing behind every misunderstanding. Assuming there are no serious issues such as drug use, adultery, and/or abuse that require the immediate intervention of a counsellor, there are a few things a married couple can consider to help their relationship.

Remember what marriage is about (Matthew 19:5). Marriage is not about tax advantages, sex, getting needs met, or even parenting. It's about two people joining every aspect of their lives together. Becoming one flesh and being unified in the stuff of life and the goals for the future. Far too often we forget, and make marriage about filling some personal need so we can go off and do what we want with the rest of our life. To restore your marriage, get back to the basics of a shared life.

Acknowledge and recognize your differences—then have the grace to consider when you might be wrong (Matthew 5:23-26). One of the biggest problems married couples have is that we expect our partner to think like we do. We forget that everyone has a different upbringing which leads to different expectations as to what family life should look like. If we can pull back from our own paradigms, we may find that our mate's family did a few things right that, if integrated into our own relationship, might even heal wounds from our past. It is not healthy for partners to unthinkingly insist on their own way of doing things. God joins a man and a woman together; the new unit will reflect some of the aspects of each of their pasts, but the couple should not be chained to any single spouse's expectations.

Forgive, forgive, forgive (Matthew 18:21-22). One of the most important characteristics of a restored marriage is the ability to forgive. If we can acknowledge our differences with our spouse and allow ourselves to see them as they really are instead of how we have them imagined in our minds, we will find it much easier to forgive. Inaccurate perceptions lead to unrealistic expectations, which result in shame and resentment. If we see our mate as they are, however, we can be grateful for the unexpected blessings they bring to the relationship.

Communicate fearlessly but gently; listen thoughtfully without defensiveness (James 1:19). When God formed Adam and Eve, He could have made them telepathic. He could have made them communicate by changing the colour of their skin. But, for whatever reason, He made them to connect through language.

Language, like everything else on earth, has been seriously damaged by sin. Even two native speakers of the same dialect use words in different ways. It's imperative to be patient when communicating. It's equally as important to know your mate well enough to recognize when serious issues can be discussed and when things need to wait for another time—sometimes your spouse will need guidance and a different perspective, and other times support and love.

Realize you're not the only ones in the room (Ephesians 6:12). God designed marriage to be good. Anything that is good will be opposed by the enemy. That's the nature of the spiritual battle in which we live. The enemy likes divorce and discord, and he is not passive. He likes to plant whispers of accusation in our ears that we unconsciously attribute to our mate. Communication and prayer will go a long way in shutting this down. If we are humble enough to lower our defences and work with our spouse, it will restore our marriage and protect our family. If we shore up our personal defences, we'll leave the relationship open for spiritual attack.

Seek advice from others (Proverbs 15:22). Marriage was created by God, and He can restore it, but sometimes He uses other people to help. Find a mentor, a Christian counsellor, or go to your pastor. There is nothing we can face that someone else hasn't triumphed over. Just be sure the counsellor really wishes to help, and not just add fuel to the flames; a counselling or mentoring session should end in encouragement and determination, not hopelessness and increased bitterness.

Concentrate on your own relationship with God. First John is an entire book dedicated to the result of a personal relationship with Jesus: we love others. We can't love others sacrificially if we don't get that love from God. We can't be filled with God's love if we neither know Him nor obey Him. Abide in Christ and He will equip you to love, forgive, listen, pray, and fight for your spouse. We can't "fix" our spouse. But our marriage will go a long way toward restoration when we allow Jesus to fix us.

IN MARRIAGE HOW DO THE TWO BECOME ONE FLESH?

God's definition of marriage can be found in Genesis 2:24:

"Therefore a man shall leave his father and his mother and hold fast to his wife, and they shall become one flesh." In the Bible, the Hebrew basar is often translated as "flesh," but however it is interpreted, it always refers to the physical part of humanity. What does it mean, then, that a man and woman become "one flesh" in marriage?

The most obvious way is through sex. This is borne out in 1 Corinthians 6:16 when Paul says even a man with a prostitute becomes one flesh with her. The act of sex is a manifestation of "one flesh" physically and a metaphor for the other ways a married couple joins together.

Much of the physical part of life involves maintenance—feeding, housing, repairing. A man and woman become one flesh in marriage when they share these things as a unit. A man is called to leave his parents—to step out of their home and provision—and become one flesh with his wife. As husband and wife work together in the stuff of life, they become united, and may even start to look like each other.

The flesh is also how we actively respond to what Jesus has done for us. God has prepared good works ahead of time for us to accomplish (Ephesians 2:10). As "one flesh," a married couple coordinates their efforts to ensure they get the work done—both as individuals and as a team. As any couple surrounded by kids, church, work, and friends knows, husbands and wives cannot fulfil their God-given duties unless they work together.

Beyond practical and spiritual matters, we need to realize that our flesh belongs to our spouse (1 Corinthians 7:4), and the way we treat our body needs to reflect the respect we have for our spouse. As trivial as it may sound, things like fitness, hair styles, and tattoos should always be considered with your spouse in mind. Falling into poor health through negligence directly affects the lifestyle of your spouse. Asking for input regarding clothes and hair shows that you care how your spouse sees you. This also applies to physical behaviour. It is disrespectful to flirt, dress revealingly, or in any other way use your body and actions to infer that you are not one flesh with your spouse.

The world is going to try to pull all of this apart. It's going to say that your body is your own, to use and treat as you see fit. It's going to insist you have to look a certain way or do certain things with your body in order to fit in. It will also lure you away from the united home life in the name of freedom, independence, and what you "deserve." Instead, God says that, in marriage, a couple becomes one flesh, to live together, honour each other with their bodies, and serve Him with their combined lives.

IS SEX INTENDED ONLY FOR PROCREATION OR CAN MARRIED COUPLES HAVE SEX JUST FOR PLEASURE?

First, the obligatory message: The Bible is clear that God designed people to have sex only within the context of marriage. Sex outside of marriage is wrong, whether it is for pleasure or any other purpose (1 Corinthians 6:18).

Nowhere does the Bible prohibit sex for pleasure. In fact, the Song of Solomon roundly approves of sex for pleasure. The origin of the church's stance against sex for pleasure is a bit convoluted and not well documented until thesixteenth century. The Council of Trent (1546) declared that amour concupiscentiae, or sensual longing (i.e.: lust), was not sin in and of itself but did have thepotential to lead to sin. Eventually, the Catholic Church formally decided that sex for the sole purpose of pleasure was not appropriate. Not necessarily because of the birth control issue, although they insist that every sexual encounter must be open to the possibility of pregnancy, but because the sex act is a worshipful expression of the love, self-sacrifice, and union of the marriage relationship.

This is deeper and richer than sex for pleasure, and it is certainly biblical to appreciate sex as a physical manifestation of God's statement that "they [the husband and wife] shall become one flesh" (Genesis 2:24). This point of view is also supported by 1 Corinthians 7:3-5. Individuals who seek sex merely for physical pleasure—even within a marriage—are not exemplifying the spirit of mutual submission God intended. Sex should be a part of and a result of a loving marriage relationship, not merely a physical release.

But when the topic of "sex for pleasure" is broached in modern times, it is usually within the context of birth control, and here the Bible has little to say. As has been explained in my bother other books on man and woman, the Bible is not against the judicious use of birth control. In addition, nowhere does the Bible state that a physically infertile couple must not have sex. In that way, it is perfectly allowable for a couple to have sex for reasons other than the attempt to have a child.

HOW OFTEN SHOULD MARRIED COUPLES HAVE SEX?

The Bible doesn't mention how often a married couple should have sex. Undoubtedly, it will be a function of proximity, the stage in life, and even logistics. In general, spouses should communicate with each other and reach an agreed- upon resolution. One possible compromise is if one spouse initiates and the other refuses, the spouse who refused is obliged to re-initiate within twenty-four hours. First Corinthians 7:4 explains that spouses have both the right to enjoy each other's bodies and the responsibility to respect each other's wishes. A healthy sex life discourages sin as the couple learns to be satisfied with each other and grows closer.

God designed sex to be an important part of a marriage relationship. Not absolutely mandatory, as some couples will experience extended periods apart or physical problems that will make sex impossible. But important nonetheless. First Corinthians 7:5 exhorts us to not deprive each other. If a couple's schedule is such that they are just too tired or don't have time, the couple needs to address the schedule. It is not scriptural to let this issue slide. Another sadly common issue is painful intercourse. For the health of the marriage, if one or the other spouse finds intercourse physically painful, he or she should seek help from a doctor or counsellor.

HOW IMPORTANT IS PHYSICAL ATTRACTION WHEN LOOKING FOR A SPOUSE?

Of course, everyone wants to be attracted to the person they marry, and what's more, they want their spouse to find them attractive. Physical intimacy is a central part of marriage, and physical attraction plays a role in that. Physical beauty and desire are not just things that the world celebrates, but the Bible does, too. The book of Song of Solomon is a love poem in which the bride and groom sing their desire for and attraction to one another. Where we tend to go wrong is when we elevate beauty in a spouse to a higher place of importance than is right. Physical attraction is important, but it is nowhere near most important. Physical beauty fades over time (Proverbs 31:30), not to mention the other physical issues that come with injury, disease, or aging. This is why the Bible puts emphasis on a person's character over their looks.

When looking for a spouse, your first concern should be his or her character rather than initial physical attraction. The Bible tells women to focus on the beauty of their heart rather than their outside beauty (1 Peter 3:3–5). The same would apply to men in principle. The Bible does acknowledge that there is some value to staying fit, but godliness has value in every area of our lives (1 Timothy 4:8). When looking for a spouse, your focus should be on the beauty of their heart and their godliness (or lack thereof). You need to find someone who will be a help when you experience tragedy and loss, someone who won't crumble under the pressures of life because they are standing on the rock of Jesus Christ. You aren't looking for someone who looks great next to you in photos; you are looking for someone who will be committed to Christ and to you. A person's heart and character is the source of true beauty, not their physical appearance.

Another danger of putting physical attraction too high on the list of what you are looking for in a spouse is that you might pass over some of the best people. You might miss the person who would be a wonderful father or mother, the person who you connect with on a deeper level than attraction, the person who would become your best friend, or the person you would enjoy the rest of your life with. This is not to say you should marry someone you don't find attractive just because he or she is a good person, but it is to say that attractiveness should not betop of your list of attributes to look for in aspouse.

HOW CAN I PREPARE MYSELF FOR MARRIAGE?

As Christians our first priority in life is to worship God in all that we do. First Corinthians 10:31 declares, "So, whether you eat or drink, or whatever you do, do all to the glory of God." We are to love God above all else and to obey His commands. When we accept Christ as our Saviour, God begins a process of transforming us and moulding us into a new creation. This transformation does not happen overnight, but if we continue to draw close to God, little by little we will become less like the world and more like Him.

In order to prepare ourselves for marriage, we can follow the same steps we take in preparing ourselves for an eternity with God. The most important thing we can do is to worship Him and obey Him. When we are aligned with God's will He can work in us to accomplish His purposes for our lives and His kingdom. As we mature in our faith, we will become more proficient in being faithful, serving others, loving unconditionally, and humbling ourselves in submission to God's will. God will heal our brokenness and refine us into better people. Every day we will begin to embody more and more the biblical description of godly men and women, and we will be equipped with the things necessary for being godly husbands and wives. Consequently, a biblical marriage exemplifies Christ's relationship with His Church (Ephesians 5:22–33).

While our spiritual growth is the most important preparation for marriage, there are a few other practical steps you can take to prepare yourself for your future spouse. First, you should pray for your future spouse even before you have met him or her. God knows what you need, but He loves to hear it directly from you. Pray for your spouse's relationship with God to be strengthened as well. Next, you should talk to married couples for advice and encouragement. They can provide you with priceless guidance and pre-marital counselling. Also, work on improving all aspects of your life. Be an active participant in the transformation God is unveiling. This could mean you need to make wise financial decisions to get out of debt or make healthier habits surrounding eating and exercising. Maybe you need to deal with things you are holding onto from your past or be willing to accept the realities of your future spouse's past. Finally, go live each day abundantly in Christ.

WHAT DOES THE BIBLE SAY ABOUT BEING A GODLY WIFE?

Proverbs 31 provides a beautiful depiction of the ideal godly wife. Although the woman in the proverb is fictional, she serves as a timeless model of a wife that pleases God. No woman is perfect, but through following the Proverbs 31 example of fearing God and allowing the Holy Spirit to work within her, all women can grow to become mature, godly women.

In order to understand what it means to be a godly wife, first we must understand what it means to be godly. When we accept Christ as our Lord and Saviour we are given the Holy Spirit. The Holy Spirit begins working within us to transform us into the new creation God wants us to become. Galatians 5:22–23 describes the work of the Holy Spirit within us as: "But the fruit of the Spirit is love, joy, peace, patience, kindness, goodness, faithfulness, gentleness, self-control ..." God created us in His image and these are all attributes of His character that He is developing within us.

Both men and women can embody the godly characteristics described in Galatians. Proverbs 31, however, demonstrates how these characteristics uniquely manifest themselves through a wife's role in marriage. The first characteristic we see of a godly woman in Proverbs 31 is that she is faithful to her husband (Proverbs 31:11–12). She is someone he can count on to support him. Next, we are told that she is hardworking (Proverbs 31:13–19, 24, 27). She looks after her family and takes responsibility instead of being lazy. In addition, she is resourceful and applies her entrepreneurial skills to start a business. She has a servant heart and cares for others (Proverbs 31:20). She is aware of her needs and takes care of herself so that she can continue to effectively care for others (Proverbs 31:22). Also, she is strong, dignified, confident, wise, and kind (Proverbs 31:25–26). These attributes gain her the respect of her husband and children. Finally, we are told she is a woman who fears the Lord (Proverbs 31:30).

While all of the characteristics demonstrated in Proverbs 31 are valuable, the most important is that a godly woman fears the Lord. It is important that a woman makes her husband a priority even above her own children. Yet her number one priority should always be God. Marriage is a symbol of the relationship between the Church and Christ (Ephesians 5:31–32); therefore, Paul states, "Wives, submit to your own husbands, as to the Lord" (Ephesians 5:22). When wives submit to the leadership of their husbands out of respect and trust, they exemplify the posture we should have as believers before Christ. In doing so, they set an example of the faith God desires from His followers for their husbands, children, and everyone around them.

DOES MARRIAGE IMPEDE ONE'S RELATIONSHIP WITH GOD?

Paul addresses how marriage might impact one's relationship with God in 1 Corinthians 7. He writes that he wants people to serve the Lord "free from anxieties" (1 Corinthians 7:32). As he says, "the married man is anxious about worldly things, how to please his wife, and his interests are divided. And the unmarried or betrothed woman is anxious about the things of the Lord, how to be holy in body and spirit. But the married woman is anxious about worldly things, how to please her husband" (1 Corinthians 7:33–34). Naturally, those who are not married have more ability to serve the Lord without the added concern of a spouse or children. Because of the freedom to serve Christ that exists in singleness, Paul says, "I wish that all were as I myself am," i.e., single (1 Corinthians 7:7). He also clearly says that this is his (Spirit-guided) opinion, not a command from the Lord (1 Corinthians 7:6). Both marriage and celibate singleness are affirmed throughout the Bible; neither situation means a person is closer to or further from God.

In 1 Corinthians 7 Paul is not saying that marriage is a bad thing, or that marriage hinders one's relationship with God. Marriage is a good thing created by God (Genesis 2:24). He structured the continuing of the human race through marriage and the bringing up of children through the context of family. God created marriage as an intimately sacrificial way we can walk out love and as a means of sanctification. Paul has a high view of marriage as we see in Ephesians: "Wives, submit to your own husbands, as to the Lord. For the husband is the head of the wife even as Christ is the head of the church, his body, and is himself its Saviour. Now as the church submits to Christ, so also wives should submit in everything to their husbands. Husbands, love your wives, as Christ loved the church and gave himself up for her, that he might sanctify her, having cleansed her by the washing of water with the word, so that he might present the church to himself in splendour, without spot or wrinkle or any such thing, that she might be holy and without blemish. In the same way husbands should love their wives as their own bodies. He who loves his wife loves himself" (Ephesians 5:22–28). This view of marriage is sacrificial on both parts as husband and wife are called to love each other and submit to the roles to which Christ has called them. Paul is not saying that marrying is a bad thing or a lesser thing. It is a different thing, and one's focus in ministry is different because of it. Your husband or wife is often the one God will use to sanctify you the most, which means that your spouse is your primary ministry.

Because marriage is such a life-sacrificial thing, Paul expresses that marriage might not be the wisest thing for everyone. He writes, "To the unmarried and the widows I say that it is good for them to remain single, as I am. But if they cannot exercise self-control, they should marry. For it is better to marry than to burn with passion" (1 Corinthians 7:7–8). The single person is able to sacrifice any and every part of their lives for other people without having to worry about neglecting their spouse or their children. For example, someone who believes God is calling him to missions in a dangerous country might have an easier time giving himself to God's calling on his life without a wife or children. On the other hand, perhaps partnering with a wife who is similarly called will be more effective. Each person should seek out what God is calling him or her to, and see from there if marriage fits the calling God has on his or her life (1 Corinthians 7:17).

While it seems single people may be more easily able to serve in ministry or to have more time to spend developing an intimate relationship with God through things like Bible study and prayer, this does not mean that married people are ineffective in ministry outside of their marriage nor that marriage impedes their relationship with God. In fact, Paul affirms, "Do we not have the right to take along a believing wife, as do the other apostles and the brothers of the Lord and Cephas?" (1 Corinthians 9:5). In 1 Timothy 3 and Titus 1 Paul gives qualifications for elders in churches. In part, the way such a man manages his own household (i.e., how he is with his wife and children) will be indicative of whether he can care for God's church. So clearly there is ample opportunity for those who are married to effectively serve the Lord both within and outside their own family. In fact, when done correctly, a marriage relationship can help both husband and wife draw closer to God. Each spouse can encourage the other in the Lord, they can seek God's will together, and they will learn and experience different aspects of God's love as they strive to love one another well.

There are benefits and hardships to both singleness and marriage. It is not singleness or marriage in themselves that cause a hindrance to our relationship with God. Rather, it is our own sin nature. People have the infamous ability to turn any good thing into an idol, and singleness and marriage are no exception. Singleness can negatively affect your relationship with God if you see it as an opportunity for selfishness and self-indulgence, rather than as a gift from God. Marriage can hinder your relationship with God if you value it over God. If you are seeking all your affirmation, all your belonging, all your meaning or your purpose from your spouse, you have put something in the way of your relationship with God. Another way marriage might hinder one's relationship with God is if one spouse is not a believer or one spouse is committed to earnestly following the Lord when the other is not. But this could also be an opportunity for the believing spouse to draw closer to God. Loving your wife or husband doesn't have to get in the way of loving God. Rather, you can learn to love your spouse because you love Christ and are changed by the gospel. While a married person's life is lived in part for their spouse, a married Christian can still put his or her spouse above themselves while living their life wholly for Christ. In the best of situations, a married couple will find that the benefits of faithful companionship serve to strengthen their relationship with God; they can build one another up and be a mutual encouragement, better together and stronger in the Lord because of the influence of their spouse (Proverbs 27:17; Ecclesiastes 4:9–12; Hebrews 10:24–25; 1 Peter 3:1–7).

MARRIAGE IS A GEM

Marriage Is a GEM. Marriage as our creator designed it, is like a precious gem. While it takes only a few minutes to get married, building a marriage takes a life time. Marriage as our creator designed it, is like a precious gem. While it takes only a few minutes to get married, building a marriage takes a life time. It takes time for two people from 2 completely different backgrounds to become fused together as one in a marriage.

Marriage should become stronger under pressure. Like a diamond, which is transformed and refined under pressure, so should your marriage be strengthened under external pressure. The harder things get, the stronger your marriage should grow. Marriage fuses two different people into one.

Building a strong marriage takes time, patience and hard work. One of the hardest adjustments a person faces when getting married is moving from a single lifestyle to a married lifestyle. Let's be real! People don't change overnight.

When you marry someone, you are marrying more than just a person, but a complete individual with different backgrounds and life experiences than yours. That is why it is now so hard for you to understand this person who is now sharing your bed and personal space. Then you discover that you see things quite differently from the other person, and this causes lots of stress and conflict in your relationship.

Adjusting to these differences is critical to marital survival. All of us filter what we see and hear through the lens of our own experiences. Personal tragedy, physical or sexual abuse, quality of family life when growing up, educational level, faith or lack of, are just a few of the things that affect the way we view the world around us. They help shape our expectations of life and influences how we interpret what other people say or do to us.

All of us enter relationships bringing our own emotional, psychological or spiritual baggage on some level. Whatever our spouse says to us, we hear through the filter of our own history and experiences. Therefore, understanding and adjusting to this requires a lot of time and patience.

Rarely will we find anything of true value simply lying on top of the ground. The "good stuff" is most often found deep down where we have to work to get at it. A good marriage is something we have to work at. It doesn't just happen by accident. Just as precious diamond is the final result of a long an intensive process, so is marriage. Marriage is a process. A fusion of 2 distinct and different elements into one.

IS MARRIAGE GOD'S IDEA?

Marriage is indeed God's idea therefore marriage is a good idea. God created and designed marriage. Marriage was not designed by society or government therefore the person with the overall authority over marriage is God and not man. God established and designed marriage restrictions. Contrary to much of today's contradictory teaches in the twenty first century, marriage has never been and will never be a man or a woman's concept. Although human come up with different concepts of marriage the author of marriage is God alone. Marriage has always been a divine origin and will always be.

MARRIAGE IS STILL GOD'S IDEA

Remember, God Himself instituted and ordained marriage at the very beginning of human history. In the Constitution of the book of Genesis and the second chapter. God laid out the details of a suitable helper for Adam the man.

Constitutional Scripture: Genesis 2:20-22.So Adam gave names to all cattle, to the birds of the air, and to every beast of the field. But for Adam there was not found a helper comparable to him. 21) And the Lord God caused a deep sleep to fall on Adam, and he slept; and He took one of his ribs, and closed up the flesh in its place. 22) Then the rib which the Lord God had taken from man He made into a woman, and He brought her to the man.

Focus Point: From the offset, God established marriage as a permanent relationship, the union of two separate people; a man and a woman, into one flesh. Adam stated that Eve was a bone of his bones and flesh of his flesh. And that she shall be called a woman because she was taken out of Adam. Marriage is meant to mirror that kind of a relationship between man and a woman.

Constitutional Scripture: Geneses 2:23. This is now bone of my bones and flesh of my flesh; she shall be called woman, because she was taken out of Man.

Focus Point: Now, one flesh is not simply the gluing of two people; but rather the "fusion" of two distinct elements in to one. If I were to glue two pieces of wood together, they would be considered bonded, not fused. In essence, they still would remain two separate pieces of wood, just bonded by glue. But with a sufficient amount of heat or pressure the bond would beak or come apart.

Now, it is different when something is fused together. When two elements are fused into one, they become inseparable. Now I want you to note: A force of sufficient magnitude may destroy them, but it will never separate them.

Please note: A man and a woman who have become "one flesh" under God's design for marriage cannot be separated without suffering great damage or even destruction.

Focus Point: When God ordained that man and the woman should "become one flesh" God had a permanent lifelong relationship in mind; but man's sin of disobedience disrupted the process.

Constitutional Scripture: Mark 10:5-9; And Jesus answered and said to them, "Because of the hardness of your heart he wrote you this precept. 6) But from the beginning of the creation, God 'made them male and female.' 7) 'For this reason a man shall leave his father and mother and be joined to his wife, 8) and the two shall become one flesh'; so then they are no longer two, but one flesh. 9) Therefore what God has joined together, let not man separate."

It was because a man and a woman's heart were hard that Moses wrote us this law, Jesus replied. ''But at the beginning of creation God' made them male and female'. 'For this reason a man will leave his father and mother and be united to his wife, and the two will become one flesh'. So they are no longer two, but one. Therefore what God has joined together, let man not separate'' (Mark 10:5-9).

Focus Point: If marriage was of a human origin, then human beings would have the right to set the standard. They would also have the right to set it aside whenever they chose to do so. But since God is the One who instituted marriage, He alone has the authority to do away with it. This He will not do, for the Constitution is quite clear: marriage is a God ordained institution that involves the joining of a man and woman as "one flesh" in a lifelong relationship. Keep in mind, this institution will last as long as human life lasts on earth. Only in the life to come will marriage be dispensed with.

MARRIAGE IS A FOUNDATION INSTITUTION BY GOD

The institution of Marriage is one of the most influential social organisation. It serves as a foundation for other social systems like home and family which play the crucial part in shaping up the life of individuals as well as the society on the whole. The first institution God introduced to man after singleness (creating man and a woman as singular) was marriage. Family is the foundation of a healthy family. Marriage is the foundation of family even before other institutions such as church, schools and other social gatherings. Marriage is a social institution, not just a private relationship. Marriage is not simply a private arrangement. It is also a social institution. As mentioned, no other form of relationship – friendship for example – is given the status of an institution.

MARRIAGE IS NOT JUST A SOCIAL CONSTRUCT, BUT A CULTURAL UNIVERSAL

How evolutionary biologists acknowledge that male-female bonding in lasting pairs was the critical step in human evolution and is something built into us by nature. Marriage reinforces and disciplines human biology, in the interests of society.

Marriage in Australia is defined in law as "The union of one woman and one man, voluntarily entered into for life". That is the time-honoured understanding of marriage for hundreds of generations of our ancestors.

However, marriage goes much deeper than any legal convention or social tradition: it is a social response to a timeless biological reality. The biological pair-bond of man and woman is nature's foundation for human life – as with other mammals – and is not a social fad to be cut to shape according to the fashion of the day. Marriage is given to us in nature; our law simply reflects reality.

Society has a vested interest in stable marriages, because human young require prolonged nurturing. The cultural phenomenon of marriage is present in every society from the earliest recorded history (with rare aberrations that merely prove the rule) while the notion of 'homosexual marriage' is a uniquely post-modern illusion. All cultures take the biological 'given' of the natural pair-bond and reinforce it with customs and ceremony to achieve the social goal of a stable family unit.

Anthropologist Claude Levi-Strauss calls marriage "a social institution with a biological foundation". He notes that throughout recorded history the human family is "based on a union, more or less durable, but socially approved, of two individuals of opposite sexes who establish a household and bear and raise children."

The timeless anthropological purpose of marriage is to bind a feral-by-nature male to his mate and his child – so necessary, historically, for the protection of the pregnant woman and vulnerable children, and for the economic viability of the family unit. Marriage exists in all societies at all times because infants from ancient Egypt to modern Ecuador need the passionately patient love and labour of both their mother and their father.

Marriage mattered to the earliest recorded human societies, because marriage creates order out of chaos: it goes some way to civilising male sexual behaviour, protecting women, ensuring stable nurturing of children, and knitting society together through kinship's 'blood and belonging'.

Ancient legal codes – like the laws of Hammurabi in Babylon around 1750 B.C., or Dadusha in the same region a century earlier – elaborate the social conditions for valid marriage, and for justice in the event of violating the marriage vows. King Dadusha, for example, specifies the social requirements of formal celebrations and a public contract, and even obtaining consent from the in-laws. The elaborate historical customs around marriage are every society's way of elevating mere mating behaviour amongst mammals to the dignity of a vital vocation – the honoured and indispensable life-task of forming a new family.

THE RELATIONSHIP BETWEEN CHRIST AND THE CHURCH

The relationship Jesus Christ has between Himself and the church must mirror that of a husband and a wife. The relationship must be that of mutual submission, a symbiotic respectable kind and with sacrificial type. Through reading from the first book of the bible to the last (Genesis to Revelation) the bible uses the smallest basic unity of society meaning or referring to ''house'' or '' family' 'A house is the foundation of society. It is through family both society and a nation is formed. It is also worth understanding that marriage is also the foundation of a house. A health house produces a healthy marriage and a healthy nation. A healthy family is a key to a healthy church, society and a nation. Every man or woman must focus on producing a healthy family because that will have a great impact on the current and next generations to come.

BIBLICALLY, WHAT CONSTITUTES A MARRIAGE?

We know that the simple act of having sex does not constitute a marriage. Jesus was very specific when speaking to the Samaritan woman in John 4: "…For you have had five husbands, and the one whom you now have is not your husband" (verse 18). In addition, Exodus 22:16-17 clearly distinguishes between sex and marriage. If sex was equal to marriage, there would be no fornication to speak of in the New Testament. The first time someone had sex, it would be marriage; sex with every subsequent partner would constitute adultery or polygamy.

Government validation is usually necessary for certain benefits, but the Bible does not say official recognition constitutes marriage. In much of the early history of mankind, there was no centralized government to oversee marriages. Even today, some governments have no authority over marriages, and others add requirements which are contrary to the Bible.

Although Jesus attended the wedding at Cana (John 2:1-11) and Jacob had a ceremony when he married Leah (Genesis 29:21-25), the Bible does not say that a social function constitutes marriage. In some cases, as with slaves and during times of war, it may not even be possible. Although weddings should be times of joy and celebration, God does not require that joy to be public.

There are many things that the Bible does not specifically, precisely describe, but can be determined by considering the intent and spirit of God's commands, as well as His character. This means that the Christian should take culture into consideration. For instance, we are not to dress as the opposite sex (Deuteronomy 22:5), but cultures have different clothing norms—dresses are universal for women in some ages, while jeans are appropriate in others; men may wear kilts, but it is inappropriate for them to wear a woman's skirt. The point is that no one in a particular place and time should be confused about a believer's gender.

Similarly, there should be little ambiguity as to whether a couple is married. The initiation of marriage should follow societal norms as much as possible. If government validation is required, it should be sought. If a ceremony and witnesses of some sort are expected, they should be provided. Then again, if the situation is such that a ceremony is forbidden or sex impossible, they are not scripturally required as long as it is clear that the couple is married. The only strict biblical requirement for marriage is that the couple should leave their parents and cleave to each other. Other cultural norms that do not go against any specific biblical instructions should be followed as closely as possible.

WHAT CONSTITUTES MARRIAGE? GOVERNMENT VALIDATION? A CEREMONY? SEX?

We know that the simple act of having sex does not constitute a marriage. Jesus was very specific when speaking to the Samaritan woman in John 4: "...For you have had five husbands, and the one whom you now have is not your husband" (verse 18). In addition, Exodus 22:16-17 clearly distinguishes between sex and marriage. If sex was equal to marriage, there would be no fornication to speak of in the New Testament. The first time someone had sex, it would be marriage; sex with every subsequent partner would constitute adultery or polygamy.

Government validation is usually necessary for certain benefits, but the Bible does not say official recognition constitutes marriage. In much of the early history of mankind, there was no centralized government to oversee marriages. Even today, some governments have no authority over marriages, and others add requirements which are contrary to the Bible.

Although Jesus attended the wedding at Cana (John 2:1-11) and Jacob had a ceremony when he married Leah (Genesis 29:21-25), the Bible does not say that a social function constitutes marriage. In some cases, as with slaves and during times of war, it may not even be possible. Although weddings should be times of joy and celebration, God does not require that joy to be public.

There are many things that the Bible does not specifically, precisely describe, but can be determined by considering the intent and spirit of God's commands, as well as His character. This means that the Christian should take culture into consideration. For instance, we are not to dress as the opposite sex (Deuteronomy 22:5), but cultures have different clothing norms—dresses are universal for women in some ages, while jeans are appropriate in others; men may wear kilts, but it is inappropriate for them to wear a woman's skirt. The point is that no one in a particular place and time should be confused about a believer's gender.

Similarly, there should be little ambiguity as to whether a couple is married. The initiation of marriage should follow societal norms as much as possible. If government validation is required, it should be sought. If a ceremony and witnesses of some sort are expected, they should be provided. Then again, if the situation is such that a ceremony is forbidden or sex impossible, they are not scripturally required as long as it is clear that the couple is married. The only strict biblical requirement for marriage is that the couple should leave their parents and cleave to each other. Other cultural norms that do not go against any specific biblical instructions should be followed as closely as possible.

DOES SEX EQUAL MARRIAGE? ARE UNMARRIED COUPLES WHO HAVE SEX MARRIED IN THE EYES OF GOD?

The short answer to the question of whether sex equals marriage is "no." Having sex does not make a couple married in God's eyes. Marriage is much more than just having one sex partner for the rest of your life; marriage is a total union of both persons physically, legally, and materially. To understand why having sex doesn't make a person married before God, one must understand how God views marriage and sex.

The Bible has many passages warning against sexual immorality, and fornication (sex before marriage) is included within this range of acts (Acts 15:20; 1 Corinthians 5:1; 6:13; Galatians 5:19; Ephesians 5:3; Colossians 3:5; 1 Thessalonians 4:3; Jude 1:7). Having sex with your significant other does not make you married because marriage is more than sex. Sex does not equal marriage. Marriage is the legally binding promise to give yourself wholly to another for the rest of your life. Sex before marriage is damaging because it separates sex from this promise. God, knowing the beauty and intimacy of sex, protects us from hurting ourselves when He tells us to reserve sex for marriage.

God created marriage as a covenant, and He is the one who binds the couple together (Matthew 19:6). Sex then becomes the act of that covenant by binding a man and woman together in physical and spiritual intimacy that mirrors the legal binding together of the couple (Genesis 2:24). Sex is a way of giving yourself completely to another person, and the covenant of marriage provides the freedom and safety to give oneself wholly (Matthew 19:6). This is a great promise, and because of that Paul writes that we should "Let marriage be held in honour among all, and let the marriage bed be undefiled" (Hebrews 13:4).

You may be unmarried and having sex with your partner with the full intention of loving them for the rest of your life. If so, what is stopping you from making this promise before God and before the law through marriage? Sex without marriage holds on to the option of walking away when one's needs are not being met, but this is not the covenantal love of marriage. This is love that keeps oneself first rather than one's significant other. God's desire is for us to enjoy all the love and support of intimate, committed relationships, and therefore He has given us the best way we can experience this on earth through marriage.

DOES THE BIBLE SAY ANYTHING ABOUT SEX BEFORE MARRIAGE?

God created sex as a beautiful gift for a husband and wife to enjoy within marriage. His purpose for this gift was to provide His creation with a human experience that would represent His spiritual relationship with them. Ephesians 5:31–32, quoting from Genesis 2:24, explains, "'Therefore a man shall leave his father and mother and hold fast to his wife, and the two shall become one flesh.' This mystery is profound, and I am saying that it refers to Christ and the church." Through sex husbands and wives are able to procreate and understand God's love for His children. In addition, they bring one another pleasure as God blesses and brings joy to His children. Finally, they commit fully to one another through trust and vulnerability as God asks us to commit ourselves fully to Him trusting His son Jesus Christ as our Saviour.

However, outside the boundaries of marriage sex is a sin. First Corinthians 7:2 states, "But because of the temptation to sexual immorality, each man should have his own wife and each woman her own husband." In this verse the apostle Paul refers to sex outside of marriage, including premarital sex, as sexual immorality. Throughout the Bible sexual immorality is denounced as a sin and refers to situations in which sex is used in a way other than how God intended it to be used (1 Corinthians 6:13, 18; Galatians 5:19; Ephesians 5:3; Colossians 3:5; Ephesians 5:3; Colossians 3:5; 1

Thessalonians 4:3; Jude 1:7).

Premarital sex can have many negative consequences. It can lead to unplanned pregnancies and abortions. When children are born outside of the family unit God created they will face more dysfunction and hardship than children born into a family with two parents who are committed to one another. Sex outside of marriage often increases a person's number of sexual partners because there is a lack of commitment to one person. This increases the likelihood a person will contract a sexually transmitted infection. Most of these infections cannot be cured and many lead to serious health problems including an early death. When two people have sex they make a unique physical connection. If that connection is lost, it leads to painful emotional baggage and broken relationships. This can cause a lack of trust and intimacy in future relationships, including a future marriage.

Most importantly, sex outside of marriage is disobedience to God. When we accept Jesus Christ as our Saviour we receive God's Holy Spirit which lives inside of us. First Corinthians 6:18–20 tells us, "Flee from sexual immorality. Every other sin a person commits is outside the body, but the sexually immoral person sins against his own body. Or do you not know that your body is a temple of the Holy Spirit within you, whom you have from God? You are not your own, for you were bought with a price. So glorify God in your body." The Holy Spirit works within us to help us follow God, and when we sin with our bodies we are in direct conflict with the work He is trying to accomplish.

The world will tell you that it is okay to have sex before marriage because sex is just about the physical pleasure. However, God created sex with the far greater purpose of creating life and a special bond between a husband and wife that symbolizes our relationship with Him. Don't let the world pollute God's purpose for sex in your life. Wait on God and the wonderful gift He has in store for you.

WHAT IS A BIBLICAL LEVEL OF INTIMACY BEFORE MARRIAGE?

Those who ask this question are usually looking for guidelines regarding physical boundaries in dating. However, intimacy is a much broader issue than physicality. A dictionary definition of intimacy talks about close friendship, deep emotional connection, and sexual involvement. To be intimate with someone is to be close to him or her, to reveal private information, to feel linked together. Intimacy includes emotional and spiritual connectedness as well as physical connection. Dating couples grow more and more intimate as they become more serious about the relationship. If proper boundaries are not established, increasing intimacy can have some undesirable results – such as feelings of abuse or betrayal following a break-up, loss of appropriate personal boundaries without a commensurate commitment, and beginning to become one before the couple actually belongs to one another. With this in mind, let's explore some boundary guidelines.

Physical: It is difficult to provide solid physical boundaries that apply to every dating relationship. Depending on one's culture and one's typical physical contact with others, physical boundaries may vary. For instance, some people hug everyone they know. This is not a sign of intimacy or love so much as it is a greeting. For others, hugging is an intimate gesture. It is also important to look at the degree to which the physical touch is carried out. There is a difference between a hug of greeting and a long embrace. Each person should be aware of the meaning he or she attaches to certain gestures when considering appropriate boundaries. It is also wise to be aware of whether certain physical touches lead a person to desire more intimate touch. For example, does a hug of greeting quickly lead to a make-out session? Recognizing personal healthy boundaries is the first step, but physical boundaries should be mutually established prior to physical contact. In the heat of the moment, it is difficult to stop a kiss that is later regretted. If both parties know the limits beforehand, maintaining boundaries becomes easier. Boundaries for physical touch should be a matter of prayer and discussion. The partner with the stricter boundaries should set the norm for the couple.

All that being said, there are certain physical boundaries that are clearly biblical. These are not a matter of personal meaning or choice. It is inappropriate to have sex, in any form, prior to marriage. It is also inappropriate to be naked in one another's presence. Sex is a gift from God that is meant for a married couple to enjoy (Proverbs 5:19; Song of Solomon; 1 Corinthians 7:1-4; Hebrews 13:4). Ephesians 5:3 says, "But sexual immorality and all impurity or covetousness must not even be named among you, as is proper among saints." The New International Version puts it this way, "But among you there must not be even a hint of sexual immorality, or of any kind of impurity, or of greed, because these are improper for God's holy people." Anything in a premarital relationship that hints of sexual immorality – like dry sex, foreplay, nudity, sleeping in the same bed, pornography, and the like – is unacceptable.

Emotional: Often, dating couples who have chosen to abstain from physical intimacy still struggle with emotional intimacy. Emotional intimacy occurs when couples share their inner thoughts with one another and rely on one another for emotional support. To an extent, dating couples will become increasingly emotionally intimate. This is a natural progression even of friendship. As people begin to know and trust one another, they become more deeply emotionally linked. However, it is wise for couples to continue to guard their hearts. Dating implies no long-term commitment. When couples find their only emotional support in one another, they set themselves up for heartbreak. There should be private portions of a heart that a person shares only with his or her spouse.

Spiritual: Some well-intentioned Christian couples begin devotionals or prayer times with one another. These are both great practices, but they also need boundaries. Our relationship with God is perhaps the most intimate thing we have. When we invite others into this, we are inviting them into intimacy. One way married couples strengthen their relationship is by praying together. Certainly, dating couples should pray together. But the manner in which they pray should preserve their personal boundaries. Married couples can pray as one unit before God. Dating couples are still two individuals.

First Thessalonians 4:3-7 says, "For this is the will of God, your sanctification: that you abstain from sexual immorality; that each one of you know how to control his own body in holiness and honour, not in the passion of lust like the Gentiles who do not know God; that no one transgress and wrong his brother in this matter, because the Lord is an avenger in all these things, as we told you beforehand and solemnly warned you. For God has not called us for impurity, but in holiness." (See also Colossians 3:5 and Galatians 5:19-24). While this passage primarily applies to physical boundaries, it can also apply to other areas of intimacy. In essence, Paul is saying that we need to learn to control ourselves. We are not to take advantage of others – whether it's taking physical liberties or pressing for another type of intimacy. We are told not to wrong each other in matters of intimacy. Dating couples do not have the commitment that married couples do. They have not yet been made one (Mark 10:8) and are no more attached to one another than friends. Dating couples should honour one another by respecting boundaries. Though dating couples are deepening their relationships and learning whether they are compatible for marriage, they should not act as though they are married. Certain gifts are reserved for marriage only.

It has often been said that you should date as if you are dating someone else's future husband or wife. What level of intimacy would you want your future spouse to have had with a previous boyfriend or girlfriend? Many people regret being too intimate before marriage, but you will never regret not being intimate enough.

MONOGAMOUS IN BIRD LIFE IS LIKE MARRIAGE ;A MAN AND A WOMAN MUST LEARN FROM THEM

Monogamy is surprisingly common among birds. About 90 percent of bird species are considered monogamous -- but, to be fair, a bird's definition of monogamy is surprisingly liberal. Ornithologists have amassed enough data to debunk the romantic notion that most birds pair up faithfully for life.

Types of Monogamy

There are two types of monogamy in birds: social monogamy and sexualmonogamy. Socially monogamous birds select a "spouse" to help raise their young, but will mate with other birds. The pairing is frequently short-lived. Most monogamous birds are socially monogamous.

Sexually monogamous birds have one mate during the breeding season, and sometimes for life. The pair mates and parents together. Rarely do they mate with other birds.

Why Monogamy?

Forming a pair bond during the breeding season helps ensure the young will thrive. In some species, both parents take turns sitting on the eggs, guarding the nest and territory, and feeding the young. Two parents are better than one.

Social Monogamy

Social monogamy is much more common than sexual monogamy. Birds will pair up to share the responsibility of raising a clutch of eggs, even though some of the babies will not belong to the parents who raise them. Socially monogamous birds will mate with other birds, and females sometimes lay their eggs in other couples' nests.

After raising a nest of babies together, socially monogamous birds frequently "divorce" and pair up with other individuals for the next breeding cycle.

Sexual Monogamy

Sexual monogamy is rare. Zebra finches are sexually monogamous for life. They form permanent breeding pairs. Scientists believe it's more beneficial for these birds to "mate for life" because of their short lifespans. Permanent pairing eliminates the time needed to find and court a mate.

Other sexually monogamous species include most geese, eagles and swans. These birds form bonded pairs for life, but both males and females may occasionally mate with other birds. Like socially monogamous birds, the bonded pair raise all the offspring in the nest, regardless of whether or not they are the biological parent.

This is why I believe monogamous animals and birds are more challenging today than majority of humans in this modern world. They have shown the true meaning of commitment. A true expression of marriage and God's intent for us.

PRINCIPLES OF MARRIAGE 1

> God is the author of marriage therefore it is His idea

> Marriage is a foundation institutions that goes before all other society institution such as schools and other social gatherings.

> Having children is not the primary purpose of marriage

> Sex is not the primary purpose of marriage

- ➢ Marriage is like a treasurable gem; a unity of two individuals together.

- ➢ A Godly marriage has God in between man and woman hence it withstandsall crisis when tested.

- ➢ A Godly marriage is a union that creates oneness.

WHAT DOES THE BIBLE SAY ABOUT SEXUAL PURITY?

God declares that sexual relations should be only for a man and a woman in a marriage and should stay between those married people for a lifetime (Ephesians 5:31). God designed sex to be pleasurable, but also instructed that it was reserved for marriage. Despite what many cultures today advocate, sexual purity is for our own benefit. Within the boundaries of marriage, sex is a pleasurable and beautiful gift. Sexual activity outside of marriage is a perversion of something God made good.

There are many Scripture passages about sexual purity, but 1 Thessalonians 4:3–5, 7 encapsulates much of God's directive on the subject: "For this is the will of God, your sanctification: that you abstain from sexual immorality; that each one of you know how to control his own body in holiness and honour, not in the passion of lust like the Gentiles who do not know God. For God has not called us for impurity, but in holiness."

Sanctification is being set apart for a holy reason—for God's purposes. When we accept Jesus as our Saviour, we are made holy and become a new creation (2 Corinthians 5:17–19). We are able to live by faith, instead of by our old sin nature (Galatians 2:20).

The Bible seems to set the lack of sexual purity somewhat apart from other sin. In the 1 Timothy passage above, sexual purity is listed as the first evidence, or step, of sanctification. Self-control over this aspect of life shows our reliance on and allowance of the Holy Spirit's work (Galatians 5:22–23). We are told to honour God with our bodies because they are a temple of the Holy Spirit (1 Corinthians 6:18–20). And it is the Holy Spirit who helps us honour Him.

Sex joins two people as one. God knows this should be reserved for marriage. First Corinthians 6:15–18 says, "Do you not know that your bodies are members of Christ? Shall I then take the members of Christ and make them members of a prostitute? Never! Or do you not know that he who is joined to a prostitute becomes one body with her? For, as it is written, 'The two will become one flesh.' But he who is joined to the Lord becomes one spirit with him. Flee from sexual immorality. Every other sin a person commits is outside the body, but the sexually immoral person sins against his own body."

God designed and created us, so He knows what is best for us. His rules, boundaries, and discipline are designed for our benefit and His glory. Sex is the most intimate and vulnerable of acts. This type of intimacy is precious within the committed relationship of a married man and woman. Remaining sexually pure protects that gift. Sexual purity is not only something those who are single need to be concerned about, but it is also intended for married couples to remain faithful to each other. Sex is unique to marriage, and sexual purity does much to maintain the integrity and strength of the marriage bond.

No matter your marital state, we are all called to be sexually pure in both our actions and our thoughts. When we follow God's instruction about sexual purity, our lives and relationships will be better for us and honour Him, and our marriage bed will be kept pure (Hebrews 13:4).

HOW SHOULD A CHRISTIAN VIEW ROMANCE?

Western culture is awash with romance. Movies, books, and music engage our attention and our hearts with emotional accounts of romance. Many people enjoy vicariously living the heart-thumping, sweaty-hands relational wonderment portrayed in media. But is this romance actually good?

First, let's define what we mean by "romance." Romance is

the initial infatuation, the excitement, the wooing and being wooed, the initial attraction to another that provides so much emotion and drama. Love, on the other hand, is the long-term commitment that binds two people together. Romance has its place, but love is what Christians are primarily called to pursue.

We understand what true love is by looking to God. First John 4:9–10 says, "In this the love of God was made manifest among us, that God sent his only Son into the world, so that we might live through him. In this is love, not that we have loved God but that he loved us and sent his Son to be the propitiation for our sins."

God expresses the ultimate love—and romance. He does pursue us, He does woo us. But our relationship with God isn't always an emotional high. God's love is steadfast and it is for us. His love doesn't always feel good or exciting. But for Christians, nothing can separate us from God's love (Romans 8:38–39). Marriage is meant to be a picture of God and the church (Ephesians 5:21–33). The best romance comes with a deep and abiding love between husband and wife. When the foundation is steady, the emotional highs of romance can be fully enjoyed. When true love is present, romance takes on a richer meaning.

The Bible has much to say about love and how Christians should love others in the context of a variety of relationships. The Bible also has stories of romance. Jacob worked seven years to win Rachel, then seven more when he was tricked into marrying her sister (Genesis 29). Song of Solomon is filled with descriptions of romantic love between a bride and groom. God is certainly not opposed to romance.

However, romance becomes dangerous when we idolize it. Those first attractions and the process of falling in love is intoxicating. In fact, the same sort of chemical release happens in our brains when we "fall in love" as when people use drugs. Science tells us that the romantic sort of being in love can be sustained for about two years, maximum. After that, those sorts of feelings taper off. Ideally they are replaced with a deeper, committed love. But if a person becomes addicted to the feelings of romance, he or she may find himself or herself feeling empty and seeking another "romantic high" in an ungodly manner.

The portrayal of romance in movies, books, plays, and music often sets us up with unrealistic portrayals of romance. Our real-life relationships, sometimes full of wonder and excitement, can still seem a bit boring and pedantic comparatively. When we overdose on vicarious romance, we may set ourselves up with false expectations and needless feelings of disappointment in the real world.

Christians are called to make commitments to agape love. First Corinthians 13 describes what true love is. Romance can be fun and can be a good thing, but only when it is in the context of true, godly love.

James 1:17 tells us that "Every good gift and every perfect gift is from above, coming down from the Father of lights, with whom there is no variation or shadow due to change." Christians should seek God's wisdom regarding things of romance, and all things for that matter (James 1:5), instead of relying solely on our emotions, no matter how strong or convincing. In romance entertainment we long for the lovers to demonstrate selfless commitment to one another. We applaud the sort of heroism, vulnerability, and pursuit we see in romance. The truest heroism in love is giving to one another the same type of selfless, committed love that God shows us (1 Corinthians 14:1).

SHOULD A COUPLE WHO GETS PREGNANT BEFORE MARRIAGE GET MARRIED?

If you seek to get married in order to get right in God's eyes, don't. Though having sex outside of marriage is a sin, only the forgiveness of Jesus Christ offers you forgiveness of all your sins. Our faith in Him is what saves us, not anything we do or do not do. Romans 6:23 says, "For the wages of sin is death, but the free gift of God is eternal life in Christ Jesus our Lord." God is more interested in your relationship with Him than in you trying to right your wrongs. When you submit your life to God through Jesus, you not only make a reservation for heaven, you will also have a fulfilling life on earth.

You know that sex outside of marriage is biblically wrong. When we go against God's plan, we invite negative spiritual and physical results such as guilt, shame, regret, loss of respect for others and self, division in relationships, pain for future spouses, unplanned pregnancy, abortion, and sexually transmitted diseases.

In our current society, sex outside of marriage is commonplace. Due to the sexualisation of our culture, it appears to some that no one possesses the discipline or commitment to remain a virgin until they are married. However, many Christians, understanding and obeying God's Word and plan for our lives, wait until marriage before having sex. God's Word is unchanging and it tells us that sex outside of marriage is wrong (Matthew 15:19; 1 Corinthians 6:9, 13; 7:2; 2 Corinthians 12:21;

Galatians 5:19; Ephesians 5:3).

That being said, having sex outside of marriage can be forgiven. The Bible tells us to confess our sins to God. When we do, He will forgive us (1 John 1:9). When we admit our sin and commit to Jesus, the natural consequences of sin remain, but we are forgiven and God will help us deal rightly with those consequences.

The Bible doesn't address whether a woman who gets pregnant should marry the baby's father. Both the mother and father are obligated to ensure their children are cared for emotionally, spiritually, and financially. Ensuring the children's needs are met may look like a variety of things, including parenting together in marriage, co-parenting without marriage, adoption, etc. It is important to remember that the baby is not at fault nor a punishment. The child is still a blessing.

Anyone contemplating marriage should be sure their future spouse is committed to God's design for marriage—a lifelong, monogamous relationship that honours God. If you already planned to marry, then seek out solid, biblical pre-marital counselling. This, not your pregnancy, will help you determine what to do about marriage. Seek God's wisdom (James 1:5). Getting married does not make you right in God's eyes. God's forgiveness is what makes us right in His eyes. We then seek His wisdom for how to proceed.

WHEN IS THE RIGHT TIME FOR MARRIAGE?

The Bible does not give us the right time for marriage, neither an ideal age to marry nor a suggested length of engagement. Girls in Bible times typically married in their teens and boys a bit later, but that was cultural, not spiritual. The Bible does give specific characteristics that men and women should strive for in a healthy marriage. It would be best if these characteristics were at least understood and accepted before the wedding took place.

The right time for marriage is when both the man and the woman are prepared to leave their families and join with their new spouse (Ephesians 5:31). It may take time for individuals to feel like they are one in their marriage, that they have developed emotional distance from their parents and really bonded with their spouse. But it's imperative that both the man and woman understand that this is required for marriage, and be willing to see it through.

Men should love their wives sacrificially (Ephesians 5:25). There is nothing like a new family member—spouse or child—to show us how selfish we really are. If a man cannot sacrifice his wants and desires for the benefit of his girlfriend, it's likely not the right time for marriage.

Women should respect their husbands (Ephesians 5:33). Far too many women marry the man they can boss around. Marriage isn't an opportunity for a woman to arrange things so her needs are met. It's an opportunity for a man and woman to join together and take care of each other. If a woman doesn't respect her boyfriend, she has no business marrying him.

It may be the right time for marriage when both individuals have the maturity to make a commitment and stick to it (1 Corinthians 7:10). God created the marriage commitment (Mark 10:9). God defined marriage. When two people agree to marry, they need to understand they aren't setting the terms; God did.

Men and women should also have the humility and courage to support and provide for their spouse (Ecclesiastes 4:11-12; 1 Corinthians 7:4). We cannot be God to our partner— we cannot meet all of his or her needs. If things happen that threaten our ability to love and respect, however, we need the humility to acknowledge the problem and the courage to seek help. That help could come through a counsellor (Titus 2:4- 5), a doctor, or even simple direct communication with one another. The ability to communicate and the humility to seek help will grow as trust grows in the relationship, but the couple should understand this is a vital part of any marriage.

In addition to the heart issues, practical matters will influence the right time for marriage. Housing, income, and children are all important considerations. Not everything needs to be completely settled, but the couple should at least identify the major issues and how they plan on resolving them. Premarital counselling is vitally important, and should be sought out by every couple who plans to marry.

No one is fully "ready" for marriage, any more than we can be fully sanctified on earth. Good relationships grow and improve every year. But the realities of married life go much more smoothly when the couple's hearts are loving and respectful (Philippians 2:3-4).

WHAT SHOULD A CHRISTIAN DO IF HE OR SHE IS MARRIED TO AN UNBELIEVER?

The Bible counsels Christians to marry other Christians. When writing to the church in Corinth, the apostle Paul advised them, "Do not be unequally yoked with unbelievers" (2 Corinthians 6:14). He knew that close relationships, like marriages, between believers and unbelievers would suffer. When one side of a relationship makes decisions based on

God's truth, and the other side remains dead in sin, the relationship has many challenges. Being in such a relationship can also feel like an extra hurdle in the spiritual growth process; it can be difficult to stay strong and encouraged in Christ when the ones you are close with disregard Him. The Israelites were similarly discouraged from intermarrying with other cultures in the Old Testament so that they would not turn away and worship other gods (Deuteronomy 7:3–4). Some think the best option is to divorce, but that is far from what the Bible says about being married to an unbeliever. If you find yourself in such a situation, do not be dismayed! There is hope and encouragement for you in Christ.

If you are a Christian married to an unbeliever, continue to trust God with your marriage and in your own faith walk. Whether you became a believer after getting married or chose to marry knowing you would be unequally yoked, you can still honour God in your marriage. First, by living out God's expectations for a spouse within a marriage and second, by sharing the love of Christ with your spouse.

A God-honouring marriage is a union between a man and a woman in which they become one flesh (Genesis 2:24). They commit to spend their lives together and do not break that commitment. In a marriage a husband is to love his wife as himself and a wife is to respect and submit to her husband (Ephesians 5:22–33). By following these guidelines, you can empower your spouse to do the same and create a healthy and happy marriage.

Many spouses in the early church found themselves in this

position after becoming Christians while married to unbelievers. Paul told them, "To the rest I say (I, not the Lord) that if any brother has a wife who is an unbeliever, and she consents to live with him, he should not divorce her. If any woman has a husband who is an unbeliever, and he consents to live with her, she should not divorce him. For the unbelieving husband is made holy because of his wife, and the unbelieving wife is made holy because of her husband" (1 Corinthians 7:12–14). God does not condone divorce, though He does allow it when one spouse has committed sexual immorality (Matthew 5:32). Paul also states in 1 Corinthians 7:15 that if an unbelieving spouse chooses to divorce the believing spouse they can consent to letting them go. However, Paul strongly encourages Christians to remain committed to their unbelieving spouse.

In addition to being a God-honouring spouse, you should also be a witness of Christ's love to your husband or wife. You can share your testimony with them, pray for them, and be an example of the transformative power of Christ in your heart. Also, make it a priority to teach your children about God. Ultimately, you are not responsible for the salvation of your spouse. It is up to them to make a decision to follow Christ. However, you are in a unique position to make a significant impact. First Peter 3:1 instructs, "Likewise, wives, be subject to your own husbands, so that even if some do not obey the word, they may be won without a word by the conduct of their wives, when they see your respectful and pure conduct."

Christians who are married to unbelievers should be encouraged that God can equip them to remain faithful in their marriage and use them to glorify Himself in the eyes of their spouse. All Christians should be engaged in regular times of fellowship with God and with other believers (John 15; Hebrews 10:24–25). Especially for Christians who find themselves in an unequally-yoked marriage, it is vital to have regular times of encouragement in Christ. This is done not only through personal Bible study and prayer, but through regular attendance at church and habitual fellowship with other believers. Others in the family of Christ can help you stay strong in your walk with God, encourage you when things are difficult, join with you in prayer for your spouse, and even be witnesses to your spouse of the gospel and the truth and love of God.

WHERE DO CHRISTIANS STAND ON SO-CALLED MARRIAGE EQUALITY?

Marriage is an institution ordained by God for the blessed union of one man and one woman. Marriage was given in an act of divine love for the good of man and woman, to be the means by which a man and a woman join sexually, to procreate, and to present a picture of Christ's love to the world (Genesis 1:28; 2:18, 24; 1 Corinthians 7:2–16; Ephesians 5:23–33). The notion of marriage "equality" is that any two (or more) persons of the same sex can be joined together in the same type of God- ordained union. However, marriage is not something that is created and defined by man, so it cannot be re-created or re-defined by man. The essence of marriage just is the joining together of one man and one woman, any other union or relationship is not a marriage.

Not all professing Christians oppose the redefinition of marriage. Even some well- known television personalities and public ministers have voiced support for marriage equality. Still, most Christians hold fast to clear biblical instruction and the teachings of the historic Christian faith. These believers ground their faith in the timeless truths of Holy Scripture. They believe that God's Word is living and active, and profitable for teaching, reproof, and correction (Hebrews 4:12; 2 Timothy 3:16).

Christians are not opposed to marriage equality because they are bigoted or spiteful. Rather, Bible-believing Christians seek to live by the Word of God. They also seek to live and to work within a society and culture congruent to the way God has ordered creation. Same sex, polygamous, and other deviant relationships are demonstrably unbiblical and outside the natural order. Christians are also not opposed to marriage equality because they lack love and compassion for those who desire to live in life- long same-sex or polygamous relationships. Christians are commanded to love their neighbours, and many Christians live out this command on a daily basis toward those who wish to redefine marriage.

It is important to note that the Christian position on marriage is not for the sake of oppressing those who disagree. Their position is based on the recognition that it is God who gives moral principles and precepts, and these are given for the good of man. God is not harmed when we disobey Him, we are. It is for our own good that we obey what God has commanded regarding marriage (and many other things). It is for our own good that we grow in sanctification, holiness, in likeness to Christ. The chief purpose for man's existence is to know God in Christ and to glorify Him. And this cannot be accomplished when man chooses to live in wanton rebellion.

The rules given by God in the Bible, and written on our hearts, serve as guardrails on our lives. Despite the high opinion we have of ourselves, the Bible gives us a dead reckoning: "for all have sinned and fallen short of the glory of God" (Romans 3:23). Christians also reject marriage as a mere social construct. They do not think that marriage is something created by culture or society as a convention or means of legal pragmatism. Societies and laws frequently change, but the commands of God are grounded in His immutable nature. If marriage is an important moral issue, then not basing it on that which is transcendent and unchanging is the height of folly.

If God has spoken about marriage, and He has, then not heeding His words is the worst thing we can do. Most people like and agree with what God says prohibiting murder and theft. And they like what He says regarding loving our neighbours, helping the poor, and so forth. But they dislike that God also tells them what to do regarding sexual behaviour and marriage. From this disdain and love of autonomy comes forth a myriad of futile objections and Scripture-twisting fabrications. Contradicting God is of course wrong in principle. Opposition to God has always proved disastrous. And opposing God over the way He structured the union of man and woman, the sexual relationship, and the fundamental family unit has, and will continue to have, disastrous consequences.

Christians stand within God's will as they uphold the sanctity of biblical marriage. They choose to be on God's side and on the side of sound biblical teaching. Christians also love, pray for, minister to, work with, and earnestly desire the salvation for all lost people. Grace abounds in the Lord Jesus Christ, and the mercies of God are new every day (Lamentations 3:22–23).

WHAT DOES IT MEAN TO 'BE FRUITFUL AND MULTIPLY' IN GENESIS?

After God created animals on the sixth day, He set out to do an even greater work. God made man in His own image out of the dust of the earth. Genesis 1:27 tells us, "So God created man in his own image, in the image of God he created him; male and female he created them." Then "God blessed them. And God said to them, 'Be fruitful and multiply and fill the earth and subdue it, and have dominion over the fish of the sea and over the birds of the heavens and over every living thing that moves on the earth'" (Genesis 1:28). God's command to Adam and Eve to be fruitful and multiply meant simply that they were to have children. They could not fulfil the rest of God's plan for them—filling the earth, subduing it, and having dominion over it—if they did not first have help. After the flood, "God blessed Noah and his sons and said to them, 'Be fruitful and multiply and fill the earth'" (Genesis 9:1). It is important to note that these were not just commands given to those responsible for populating the earth, but blessings. And this blessing still stands for humanity today.

There are many implications for God's blessing to be fruitful and multiply. First we see that part of the purpose for marriage is to have children. God designed marriage as a picture of Christ and the church (Ephesians 5:21–33) to be lived out intimately before one's children so that they could begin to understand the character of God. The family also provides the unique experience of discipling a person from birth. Parents have the opportunity to live out the gospel for their children in a way that will influence their children more than anyone else in their lives.

While this is one of many purposes for marriage, it does not mean that couples who don't have children are living in sin. Couples who struggle with infertility are in no way breaking God's command on their lives. Even couples who can have children and don't are not necessarily sinning. However, married couples who are able to have children should seriously pray about having children, knowing that the Bible calls children a blessing (Psalm 127:3–5).

Similarly, God's command to be fruitful and multiply does not mean that it is God's will for every single person to get married. Jesus and Paul both say that in some cases it is better to be able to live a life of celibacy, but that not everyone is able to or called to live a life of celibacy, "only those to whom it is given" (Matthew 19:11; 1 Corinthians 7). Perhaps the clearest argument that God's blessing and command to Adam, Eve, Noah, and Noah's family is not a blanket command for every person to marry and have children is Jesus Himself. He lived a perfect and sinless life, yet Jesus never married nor did He have children.

Another implication of this verse is in the blessing to be fruitful. Throughout the Bible fruitfulness is a metaphor for the blessings that come from righteous living. The primary fruit of one's life that is referred to here is having children. While this is the primary reference of fruitfulness in God's command as given in Genesis, it does not exclude other forms of fruitfulness. God's will is for our lives to bear good fruit in all areas (Galatians 5:22–23). Consider, too, that we can be spiritually fruitful and multiply when we obey God's commands to "make disciples of all nations" (Matthew 28:19).

God's design for humanity as a whole is to have children and fill the earth. He gave people the gift of having children because He knew they would be a joy and a legacy. By being made in His image, He has blessed us with the ability to build and create, to guide and direct, and His desire is that we use these abilities to subdue creation and steward it. God's blessing on Adam and Eve, and later on Noah and his family, became the basis for our way of life and our livelihood.

CAN WIDOWS / WIDOWERS REMARRY? WHAT IS THE BIBLICAL VIEW OF REMARRIAGE AFTER DEATH OF A SPOUSE?

First Corinthians 7:39-40 gives blanket permission for remarriage after the death of one's spouse—although it is not mandatory:

A wife is bound to her husband as long as he lives. But if her husband dies, she is free to be married to whom she wishes, only in the Lord. Yet in my judgment she is happier if she remains as she is. And I think that I too have the Spirit of God.

Marriage vows are only binding while both parties live. There is no marriage in heaven (Matthew 22:30), so there is no marriage of the dead.

In the Old Testament, remarriage after the death of a spouse was usually a matter of children. After Sarah died, Abraham married Keturah who gave him six sons. God supported Levirate marriages (wherein a childless widow married her late husband's brother to provide an heir for her husband) so that a man's property would remain with his descendants and a woman would be cared for by her son (Deuteronomy 25:5-6). This ensured the woman had an option to remarry since, as a widow, she could not provide a political advantage for her father's family.

With the advent of the church, women didn't have to remarry after the death of their spouses. The church as Christ's body was impelled to provide for faithful, righteous, elderly widows who had no family support (1 Timothy 5:3-10). In a way, the church was compensating such women for the kingdom work they performed (verse 10). Older widows with family were to be cared for by their family. Younger widows, however, were not to be supported by the church. It was doubted as to whether a young widow could truly dedicate the rest of her life to God and the church, rejecting all possibility of remarrying. (There were exceptions, of course, as in Anna in Luke 2:36-37.) An older widow had a resume of sorts, showing her lifetime of prudent and godly living. Younger women were tempted not only by the thought of marriage, but also by the idleness that comes with financial stability and no direct responsibilities. Since tending a family was one of the very few career choices young women had, it was better they were occupied with that.

In a culture where the desire to be married was assumed and, for women, the idea of support without family was nearly impossible, remarriage after a spouse's death was a great attraction on a purely practical level. That is not always the case in modern times. Women do not need the protection and support of a spouse to serve God, and men never did (see: Jesus, Paul, many of the Old Testament prophets). The Bible clearly says that widows and widowers are free to remarry, but it does not say if they should. Remarriage is as much a matter for spiritual discernment as the initial marriage. It is good to be married, and it is good to be single. Only God knows which is best for each person.

DOES MARRIAGE IMPEDE ONE'S RELATIONSHIP WITH GOD?

Paul addresses how marriage might impact one's relationship with God in 1 Corinthians 7. He writes that he wants people to serve the Lord "free from anxieties" (1 Corinthians 7:32). As he says, "the married man is anxious about worldly things, how to please his wife, and his interests are divided. And the unmarried or betrothed woman is anxious about the things of the Lord, how to be holy in body and spirit. But the married woman is anxious about worldly things, how to please her husband" (1 Corinthians 7:33–34). Naturally, those who are not married have more ability to serve the Lord without the added concern of a spouse or children. Because of the freedom to serve Christ that exists in singleness, Paul says, "I wish that all were as I myself am," i.e., single (1 Corinthians 7:7). He also clearly says that this is his (Spirit-guided) opinion, not a command from the Lord (1 Corinthians 7:6). Both marriage and celibate singleness are affirmed throughout the Bible; neither situation means a person is closer to or further from God.

In 1 Corinthians 7 Paul is not saying that marriage is a bad thing, or that marriage hinders one's relationship with God. Marriage is a good thing created by God (Genesis 2:24). He structured the continuing of the human race through marriage and the bringing up of children through the context of family. God created marriage as an intimately sacrificial way we can walk out love and as a means of sanctification.

Paul has a high view of marriage as we see in Ephesians: "Wives, submit to your own husbands, as to the Lord. For the husband is the head of the wife even as Christ is the head of the church, his body, and is himself its Saviour. Now as the church submits to Christ, so also wives should submit in everything to their husbands. Husbands, love your wives, as Christ loved the church and gave himself up for her, that he might sanctify her, having cleansed her by the washing of water with the word, so that he might present the church to himself in splendour, without spot or wrinkle or any such thing, that she might be holy and without blemish. In the same way husbands should love their wives as their own bodies. He who loves his wife loves himself" (Ephesians 5:22–28). This view of marriage is sacrificial on both parts as husband and wife are called to love each other and submit to the roles to which Christ has called them. Paul is not saying that marrying is a bad thing or a lesser thing. It is a different thing, and one's focus in ministry is different because of it. Your husband or wife is often the one God will use to sanctify you the most, which means that your spouse is your primary ministry.

Because marriage is such a life-sacrificial thing, Paul expresses that marriage might not be the wisest thing for everyone. He writes, "To the unmarried and the widows I say that it is good for them to remain single, as I am. But if they cannot exercise self- control, they should marry. For it is better to marry than to burn with passion" (1 Corinthians 7:7–8). The single person is able to sacrifice any and every part of their lives for other people without having to worry about neglecting their spouse or their children. For example, someone who believes God is calling him to missions in a dangerous country might have an easier time giving himself to God's calling on his life without a wife or children. On the other hand, perhaps partnering with a wife who is similarly called will be more effective. Each person should seek out what God is calling him or her to, and see from there if marriage fits the calling God has on his or her life (1 Corinthians 7:17).

While it seems single people may be more easily able to serve in ministry or to have more time to spend developing an intimate relationship with God through things like Bible study and prayer, this does not mean that married people are ineffective in ministry outside of their marriage nor that marriage impedes their relationship with God. In fact, Paul affirms, "Do we not have the right to take along a believing wife, as do the other apostles and the brothers of the Lord and Cephas?" (1 Corinthians 9:5). In 1 Timothy 3 and Titus 1 Paul gives qualifications for elders in churches. In part, the way such a man manages his own household (i.e., how he is with his wife and children) will be indicative of whether he can care for God's church. So clearly there is ample opportunity for those who are married to effectively serve the Lord both within and outside their own family. In fact, when done correctly, a marriage relationship can help both husband and wife draw closer to God. Each spouse can encourage the other in the Lord, they can seek God's will together, and they will learn and experience different aspects of God's love as they strive to love one another well.

There are benefits and hardships to both singleness and marriage. It is not singleness or marriage in themselves that cause a hindrance to our relationship with God. Rather, it is our own sin nature. People have the infamous ability to turn any good thing into an idol, and singleness and marriage are no exception. Singleness can negatively affect your relationship with God if you see it as an opportunity for selfishness and self- indulgence, rather than as a gift from God. Marriage can hinder your relationship with God if you value it over God. If you are seeking all your affirmation, all your belonging, all your meaning or your purpose from your spouse, you have put something in the way of your relationship with God. Another way marriage might hinder one's relationship with God is if one spouse is not a believer or one spouse is committed to earnestly following the Lord when the other is not. But this could also be an opportunity for the believing spouse to draw closer to God. Loving your wife or husband doesn't have to get in the way of loving God. Rather, you can learn to love your spouse because you love Christ and are changed by the gospel. While a married person's life is lived in part for their spouse, a married Christian can still put his or her spouse above themselves while living their life wholly for Christ. In the best of situations, a married couple will find that the benefits of faithful companionship serve to strengthen their relationship with God; they can build one another up and be a mutual encouragement, better together and stronger in the Lord because of the influence of their spouse (Proverbs 27:17; Ecclesiastes 4:9–12; Hebrews 10:24–25; 1 Peter 3:1–7).

MARRIAGE IS HONOURABLE

"Marriage – An Honourable Experience". Marriage is the foundation of the family and the family is close to the heart of God. The analogy between the church and the family in Ephesians 5, shows the place of the family in the heart of God.

Marriage is very close to the heart of the Father. That is why this end-time, before Jesus returns, there will be perfection of the families of believers that will allow the power of the Word of God to bring them to the place of excellence and honour. I believe your marriage will be a part of it in Jesus' name.

In Hebrews 13:4 the Bible says: Marriage is honourable in all and the bed undefiled, the whoremongers and adulterers God will judge. Marriage is honourable not only in some things, but in all things. It is not instituted by God to bring you into a life of misery, but to bring honour to your life – spirit, soul, and body.

VOWS IN MARRIAGE

Christian Marriage Vows Unveiled Phrase by Phrase

When you are planning your wedding ceremony it is easy to get caught up in all the finer details: choosing your entourage, arranging an officiant and deciding on everything from decor to catering. And when it comes to the actual marriage vows, you may be left wondering which route to go – should you create your own words, and if so what would you say? Or perhaps you would like to go the traditional route and stay with the well known and loved phrases of the original Christian marriage vows as printed in the Book of Common Prayer. These Christian marriage vows have been joyfully and sincerely used by literally millions of couples to seal their love for one another in a beautiful covenant.

If you are not familiar with the words of the conventional Christian marriage vows or the meaning of marriage vows, this book will seek to unveil them phrase by phrase. Once you have thoughtfully considered each phrase, you will be able to enjoy and appreciate the meaning behind the Christian marriage vows that you will both be making on your wonderful wedding day. Marriage vows' meaning will make a special place in your heart.

I take you to be my wedded wife/husband

Right up front this phrase expresses the choice and decision of each partner. She is choosing him and he is choosing her. Both of you together have decided to move your relationship forward to the next level of commitment. Of all the people in the world, you are choosing each other, and this phrase is an important reminder that you are taking responsibility for your choices. It is also a beautiful expression of love which can be repeated over and over in the months and years to come as you tell each other "I took you to be my wedded wife/husband."

To have and to hold

What does to have and to hold mean?

One of the most precious aspects of a marriage relationship is to have and to hold meaning, physical intimacy. As husband and wife, you are free to express your love for one another affectionately, romantically and sexually. To have and to hold vows speaks of your expectation, that you are looking forward to enjoying each other's company in every way, be it physically, socially or emotionally, you will share every area of your lives with one another.

From this day forward

The next phrase, "from this day forward" shows that something completely brand new is starting on this day. You are crossing a threshold on your wedding day, from the state of singleness into the state of being married. You are leaving your old way of living behind and you are starting a new season or a new chapter together in the story of your lives.

For better or for worse

The next three wedding phrases underline the seriousness of your commitment, acknowledging that life has both ups and downs. Things do not always turn out the way you had hoped or dreamed they would, and real-life tragedies can happen to anyone. At this point, it should be understood that this phrase is not meant to lock someone into an abusive relationship where a marriage partner uses these words to threaten and intimidate you into remaining faithful and present, while he or she treats you badly. Both partners need to be equally committed to these Christian wedding vows, facing life's struggles together.

A SUCCESSFUL MARRIAGE DEPENDS ON KNOWLEDGE

A successful marriage depends on the application of knowledge – knowing and understanding God's principles. You must understand what it means to be a woman; you must understand what it means to be a man; you have to understand communication skills; you must understand how to manage emotions and how to handle anger; you must understand the dynamics of disagreement; you must understand how to handle unfaithfulness.

Knowledge and love; requisites of a successful marriage. Marriage is not a requirement of God. Nowhere in the Bible did God command us to marry or to be married. Marriage is a choice that one can make in his life, but it is not a requirement of God. You do not have to get married to be happy. And also do not get married to someone just because you love him. Love does not keep marriage together. A successful marriage depends on the application of knowledge – knowing and understanding God's principles. You must understand what it means to be a woman; you must understand what it means to be a man; you have to understand communication skills; you must understand how to manage emotions and how to handle anger; you must understand the dynamics of disagreement; you must understand how to handle unfaithfulness. If you do not understand those things you cannot keep your marriage. Many marriages are broken because the individuals did not have the equipment – the requisite knowledge to use to fix the situation. The most misunderstood element of a relationship is love; love is not emotions; love is a choice; love is the response to understanding the value of a thing; love is a force generated

by a decision; love is an act of the will – love is a decision; love is a debt you owe; Love is a decision to commit to meet the needs of another for life without expectation; Love is caring – anticipating a need and meeting it.

PRINCIPLES OF MARRIAGE 2

- ➢ Marriage must be unchanging no matter life challenges or consequences of a global pandemic.

- ➢ Marriage is always tested even in turmoil

- ➢ Marriage is more understood with wisdom and understanding as stated in proverbs 24:3 rather than personal feelings or emotions.

- ➢ Be committed to a marriage rather than to a person for a marriage to be successful

- ➢ God only joins what He allows

- ➢ What God has put together no man is allowed to separate

➢ Success in marriage is about the knowledge and application as you cannot apply what you do not know.

➢ Fear for God is the beginning of wisdom. Without wisdom your marriage cannot stand as the foundation of marriage is built on wisdom and understanding.

➢ Marriage is God's will

➢ Marriage is an expression of God's love for another person

➢ Marriage fulfils sexual needs and desires in a Godly way

➢ Marriage is a desire to begin a family

➢ Marriage is companionship

➢ Marriage forms a unity between a man and a woman

➢ Marriage is designed by believers those who walk by faith and not by sight.

HOW CAN I HEAL FROM THE PAIN OF BETRAYAL?

There is perhaps no greater insult to relationship than

betrayal. Betrayal robs us of a sense of security. Someone close to us has proven untrustworthy. Most of us have felt the sting of betrayal; likely most of us have even inflicted it. So what do we do about it?

There are obvious dangers in not overcoming the pain betrayal causes—losing the ability to trust, becoming a betrayer in retaliation or self-defence, not acknowledging the betrayal and thereby exposing ourselves to further hurt, emotional numbing to avoid the pain (which will eventually lead to an inability to experience joy as well). We work through the pain so that we might trust again, so that we might find the true foundation of our security.

Jesus was not immune to betrayal. Judas, one of the twelve disciples, a friend whom Jesus trusted with the group's finances, turned Him in to be crucified. What is perhaps worse is that Judas accepted thirty pieces of silver in exchange for the life of his friend (Matthew 26:14-16). He betrayed Jesus with a kiss of greeting (Matthew 26:49). Jesus knew that Judas would betray Him, yet He chose to bring the man into His inner fellowship. Jesus called Judas "friend," even after the kiss that would lead to Jesus' arrest.

On a smaller scale, Peter betrayed Jesus. The disciple who vowed to follow Jesus to death (Matthew 26:33-35), three times denied even knowing Jesus. After His resurrection, Jesus restored Peter, giving the man three opportunities to affirm his love for Jesus and confirming His trust in the disciple (John 21:15-19).

David, too, experienced the sting of betrayal. In Psalm

55:12-15 he writes, "For it is not an enemy who taunts me—then I could bear it; it is not an adversary who deals insolently with me—then I could hide from him. But it is you, a man, my equal, my companion, my familiar friend. We used to take sweet counsel together; within God's house we walked in the throng. Let death steal over them; let them go down to Sheol alive; for evil is in their dwelling place and in their heart." David was no stranger to the torment of enemies, but even that seemed less painful than betrayal from a friend. Let's look at David's response.

But I call to God, and the LORD will save me. Evening and morning and at noon I utter my complaint and moan, and he hears my voice. He redeems my soul in safety from the battle that I wage, for many are arrayed against me. God will give ear and humble them, he who is enthroned from of old, Selah, because they do not change and do not fear God. (Psalm 55:16-19)

David's first response was to experience the pain of betrayal. He did not minimize his sense of hurt. He poured it out to God. We, too, must acknowledge when we have been hurt. And then we need to share that hurt with someone who understands. God understands. Not only was Jesus betrayed in His time on earth. God has been, in a sense, betrayed by His creation. He created us that we might glorify Him and enjoy Him. Instead of fellowshipping with Him, we sinned against Him, and He had to redeem us. Because God so easily relates with our pain, we can pour out our hurt to Him in prayer. When the betrayal is deep, it can be helpful to talk with a trusted friend or counsellor as well. Be wise to refrain from gossip in doing this.

Next, David realized his behaviours needed to be altered. He recognized that he could not trust his friend in the same way. Psalm 55:20-21 says, "My companion stretched out his hand against his friends; he violated his covenant. His speech was smooth as butter, yet war was in his heart; his words were softer than oil, yet they were drawn swords." David understood his friend's true heart.

It needs to be said that not all betrayers commit their act intentionally. Judas and David's friend certainly did. Peter did not. Sometimes friends betray us simply because they are sinful human beings (just like us). It is still wise to recognize that these people may not be as trustworthy as we once believed. However, it would be unwise to paint them with a broad brush, declaring them evil and unworthy of reconciliation.

The final step in overcoming the pain of betrayal is that of forgiveness. When we forgive someone, we are really giving ourselves a gift. Especially when people intentionally inflict pain on us, our withholding of forgiveness hurts us more than it does them. To forgive someone is to give up our right to vengeance. We acknowledge that their act was wrong, we might be more careful in trusting them with certain issues, but we do not attempt to get back at them. We don't betray someone who betrayed us. Instead, like David did, we leave it in God's hands. David concludes his Psalm this way: "Cast your burden on the Lord, and he will sustain you; he will never permit the righteous to be moved. But you, O God, will cast them down into the pit of destruction; men of blood and treachery shall not live out half their days. But I will trust in you" (Psalm 55:22-23). God will take care of evildoers. And He will take care of us.

Betrayal is a robbing of security through a breaking of trust. We overcome the heartache it causes by giving our pain to God. We call the betrayal for what it is, reconsider our personal boundaries, and recognize that only God is truly trustworthy. We tell Him our pain and allow Him to handle those who would hurt us.

WHAT IS A BIBLICAL DEFINITION OF TRUE FRIENDSHIP?

Friendships can be among the most rewarding and the most frustrating relationships in our lives. From Old to New Testament, the Bible is full of friendship stories and advice. We are told that friends love at all times (Proverbs 17:17), only wound us in ways that are trustworthy (i.e., tough love; Proverbs 27:6), are more loyal than family at times (Proverbs 18:24), provide mutual edification (Proverbs 27:17), can impart wisdom (Proverbs 13:20), and they may even sacrifice themselves for us (John 15:13).

David and Jonathan are well-known for their close friendship. First Samuel 18:1-5 talks about the knitting of the two men's souls. Jonathan gave his robe and armour to David, essentially honouring David above himself and stripping himself of his kingly position (Jonathan's father was King Saul). Later Jonathan stood up for David to his father (1 Samuel 19:1-7). Jonathan risked his life for his friend (1 Samuel 20). God used the friendship to preserve David for the throne. David, too, had deep loyalty to Jonathan. Second Samuel 1:17-27 is David's lament over the death of Saul and Jonathan. Even though Saul had been an enemy to David, the new king sought out someone from Saul's family that he might show him kindness for the sake of Jonathan (2 Samuel 9:1- 13; 21:7). David's sense of loyalty to Jonathan and his gratefulness for their friendship outweighed the enmity between Saul and David.

Embedded in instructions regarding the Church is some advice about friendship. Paul told believers to be compassionate, kind, humble, meek, patient, forgiving, at peace with one another, loving, and thankful (Colossians 3:13-15). Friends also teach one another and worship God together (Colossians 3:16).

The truest friend is Jesus. John 15:12-15 says, "This is my commandment, that you love one another as I have loved you. Greater love has no one than this that someone lay down his life for his friends. You are my friends if you do what I command you. No longer do I call you servants, for the servant does not know what his master is doing; but I have called you friends, for all that I have heard from my Father I have made known to you." Friends are like-minded. They love one another with sacrificial love. They share with one another from the heart. Friends know each other well and promote one another's welfare. We are blessed to have been adopted into the family of God and to have been made friends of Jesus. In return, we are called to be good friends to one another.

According to the Bible, true friendship is characterized by love. The Proverbs, the example of David and Jonathan, instructions to the Church, and, ultimately, Jesus' example depict true friendship. A true friend loves, gives wise counsel, remains loyal, forgives, and promotes the other's welfare.

HOW CAN I OVERCOME REJECTION?

Rejection is a common and normal experience. It happens in relationships, in business ventures, and in other pursuits. We seek out a connection and are refused, or we apply for something and are denied. Rejection often causes us to question our worth as people. Even those who know Jesus as Saviour and know that their identity is in Christ and not in the opinions of others are not immune to the hurt of rejection. As painful as rejection can be, especially when it first happens, it is something we can move past, especially with God's help.

The first step is to acknowledge our emotion and share our hurt with God. Pretending that rejection did not occur or that it doesn't hurt will not do any good. God already knows. In fact, He understands our feelings more deeply than we can imagine. Look at how many rejected Jesus during His time on earth. Look at how many still reject God's offer of love and grace. God can certainly empathize with us.

After we've shared our hurt with God, we seek His comfort. This comes through prayer and through the truth of God's Word. When we belong to Christ, we are children of God (John 1:12–13). We are fully loved and nothing will ever separate us from God's love (Romans 8:31–39). He has "blessed us in Christ with every spiritual blessing in the heavenly places" (Ephesians 1:3). He "chose us in him before the foundation of the world" and "predestined us for adoption to himself as sons through Jesus Christ" (see Ephesians 1:4–10). Remembering our identity in Christ and the lavish love of God will go a long way in removing the sting of human rejection.

Sometimes rejection is the simple result of a relationship or job or other circumstance not being a good fit. It may take us aback, but we can "… know that for those who love God all things work together for good, for those who are called according to his purpose. For those whom he foreknew he also predestined to be conformed to the image of his Son, in order that he might be the firstborn among many brothers" (Romans 8:28–29). God's plans for our lives do not fail because of rejection. Rather, rejection can be an impetus for our spiritual growth and a reminder that God is sovereign (James 1:2–5; Romans 5:3–5).

Sometimes rejection is a result of something in our lives that needs to change. For example, we may be rejected for a job because we need more education. Or someone might reject us as a friend because we come across as haughty or mean. While rejection should not cause us to question our fundamental worth as humans made in God's image or as children of God in Christ, it is okay for rejection to prompt self- reflection. Ask God to guide you if there is something in your life or in your character that needs His transforming touch. Then submit to His work in your life with joy. When God reveals something in us that needs to change, it is not to shame us, but to grow us in Christ and complete His good work (Philippians 1:6; 2:12–13; 2 Corinthians 3:17– 18; 13:5).

Sometimes we are rejected because we are Christians. Jesus told His followers, "If the world hates you, know that it has hated me before it hated you. If you were of the world, the world would love you as its own; but because you are not of the world, but I chose you out of the world, therefore the world hates you" (John 15:18–19; see also Luke 10:16). We need not be offended when people reject us because of Christ. Instead, we can ask for God's heart for such people and pray that they will come to know Him. Jesus is the only Saviour (John 14:6; Acts 4:12), if people reject Him, they remain condemned (John 3:16–18). With God's perspective, the pain of rejection shifts from one of personal affront to one of sadness at their lost state and desire for them to come to know Christ.

Rejection is something we will continue to deal with throughout our lives. But it is not something that should hinder us. Instead, we can use rejection as an opportunity to experience God's comfort and be reminded of the truth and steadfastness of His love. Our worth rests squarely in God, not in the attitudes or actions of others, whether they accept us or reject us. God is the measure of truth, not the changing values and opinions of the world or those in it (John 8:31–32).

HOW CAN I HEAL FROM A BROKEN HEART / HEARTBREAK?

Broken relationships, disappointment in others, loss of a job, an unfulfilled dream, or other dire circumstances can cause heartbreak, and the pain can feel overwhelming.

Society offers many remedies for heartbreak, ranging from shopping to getting a makeover to harmful activities such as excessive drinking of alcohol, doing drugs, or jumping into a quick relationship to salve the hurt. Many of these activities and actions will only temporarily distract us from the hurt; some will cause lasting harm to ourselves and others.

Perhaps the most consistent solution society gives to deal with heartache is time. Time will help, but believers in Jesus don't have to simply wait in order to find any relief for the pain of heartbreak. We can go to God with our broken hearts and find comfort.

How? Turn your attention to God's care for your heart. God says He is interested in your heart (1 Samuel 16:7). Look at this passage from Psalm 147:2–5: "The LORD builds up Jerusalem; he gathers the outcasts of Israel. He heals the broken-hearted and binds up their wounds. He determines the number of the stars; he gives to all of them their names. Great is our Lord, and abundant in power; his understanding is beyond measure."

Set there right between God's care for His people as a nation (Psalm 147:2) and His power to create the universe (Psalm 147:4), He focuses on the individual and the very core of care for the individual (Psalm 147:3). Then, the psalm reminds us of the greatness of God, His ability, and His immeasurable understanding (Psalm 147:5). God truly does care, and He truly is amazing. Remembering this, and turning to God, can be a balm to our heartache.

Job offers us a model of how to react to heartbreak. When he loses his children, wealth, and eventually even his health, his reaction is to grieve and also to worship God (Job 1:20–21; 2:9–10). Job knew God is always faithful, and Job determined to be faithful as well. We, too, can grieve, and do so while still trusting in God and worshipping Him.

Psalm 34 also offers us an example of how to deal with a broken heart. David called upon the name of the Lord (Psalm 34:4), then reminded himself of God's nearness and help (Psalm 34:18). He concludes by expressing confidence in God's love: "Many are the afflictions of the righteous, but the LORD delivers him out of them all … The LORD redeems the life of his servants; none of those who take refuge in him will be condemned" (Psalm 34:19).

Heartbreak is a common human experience. It is quite a rare thing to put your trust in any person or circumstance and not be disappointed at some level. Every person has faults and is unable to live up to his or her own design because of sin. The fallen nature of our world means we live with disappointments and hurts. But we need not despair!

God has said that He "will never leave your nor forsake you" (Hebrews 13:5). God can comfort you (2 Corinthians 1:3–4). Second Corinthians 4:7–12 reminds us that our earthly lives are temporary and often demonstrate death, but there is life in Jesus. Instead of succumbing to the hopeless feeling that may accompany our broken hearts, we can use heartbreak to remind us that only God can truly fulfil and meet our deepest needs. Let your heartbreak drive you to God, where you will find unfathomable love.

Psalm 62:8 says, "Trust in him at all times, O people; pour out your heart before him; God is a refuge for us." Psalm 56:8 tells us that God keeps account of our tears. It is okay to be hurt and to share your heartbreak with God. Pour it out to Him; then trust Him to comfort you. Life is not over; God is at work and He is faithful to complete His good work in you (Philippians 1:6).

Be encouraged by Colossians 3:2–4: "Set your minds on things that are above, not on things that are on earth. For you have died, and your life is hidden with Christ in God. When Christ who is your life appears, then you also will appear with him in glory."

HOW CAN I HEAL FROM THE HURT OF A BROKEN RELATIONSHIP?

The hurt of a broken relationship can derail and devastate us. It can cause feelings of pain, loss, confusion, guilt, heartbreak, anger, rejection, and sadness. Although we typically think of a relationship in romantic terms, we can also have broken relationships with friends and family members. Some people try to numb the pain through antidepressants, drugs, or alcohol. Others push to move forward jumping into a new relationship, getting a makeover, or trying new things. Some find help in counselling and positive thinking and others remain stuck in their depression and anger. While time can help a person to move forward, only God can bring true healing to a broken heart.

God understands the hurt of a broken relationship better than anyone. When Adam and Eve sinned in the Garden of Eden they were separated from God. The relationship between God and His creation was broken (Isaiah 59:2). Jesus also suffered from broken relationships. He was rejected by the community He grew up in when He went to preach to them. He was betrayed by Judas, one of His closest followers. He was abandoned by the disciples and denied by Peter in the final hours of His life. He was crucified on the cross by the people He came to save (Mark 6:1–4; Matthew 26:14– 16, 75).

Yet, the very fact that Jesus suffered while on this earth is the reason we have hope. Jesus suffered, but He overcame the brokenness of the world. In doing so, He restored and redeemed the broken relationship between God and His creation. Therefore, God can restore and redeem the brokenness in our lives (Romans 8:1–39).

If you are suffering from a broken heart, turn to God. When you put your faith in Jesus, He will begin to bring healing into your life. The Bible tells us that Jesus can empathize with us (Hebrews 4:15). He knows that we need to be loved. He loves us unconditionally regardless of who we are or what we have done. When we accept Him as our Saviour, our new identity is as a child of God (John 1:12). God will comfort us and promises to never leave us (2 Corinthians 1:3–4; Hebrews 13:5; Isaiah 43:2). He transforms our thoughts and instils us with joy that is not shaken by our circumstances.

He equips us so that we can stand strong in the face of hardship (2 Peter 1:3–8; James 1–5; Ephesians 6:10–18 ;).

The most important step in the healing process is forgiveness. In order to receive forgiveness for our sins, we have to confess them to God and accept that it is only through the presence of Jesus in our lives that we can be saved (John 3:16–18; 1 John 1:9; Ephesians 2:8–9). Likewise, healing can only come into a broken relationship when forgiveness is present. We must forgive and ask for forgiveness so that both us and the other person can experience healing (Ephesians 4:32).We will experience heartbreak in this lifetime because we live in a broken world. However, one day Jesus will come back and sin will be defeated once and for all. God promises, "He will wipe away every tear from their eyes, and death shall be no more, neither shall there be mourning, nor crying, nor pain anymore, for the former things have passed away" (Revelation 21:4).

WHAT DOES THE BIBLE SAY ABOUT DEALING WITH DIFFICULT PEOPLE?

Difficult people are everywhere. Hostile, rude, mean, selfish, impatient, uncaring, and worse (Romans 1:29–31; 2 Timothy 3:1–4; Galatians 5:19–21; 1 Corinthians 6:9–11). What may be shocking to many of us is that we have and can act the same as these people. Are we always hostile, rude, mean, selfish, impatient, and uncaring? No, but we all have the seeds of all such attitudes in our hearts (Matthew 15:19; Jeremiah 17:9). Therefore, the first step in helping us deal with difficult people is understanding that we are not better than such people by nature (Ephesians 2:1–3). We live in a fallen world filled with sinful people. We must remind ourselves of this fact so that we are not surprised when we encounter difficult people, or when we find ourselves being a difficult person.

If we have received Jesus Christ, then we are forgiven for these sinful attitudes and behaviours. When we find ourselves displaying such attitudes and behaviours, we confess to God and trust that He has already forgiven us and will cleanse us (1 John 1:8–9). We make amends when possible and seek to live differently. God's forgiveness of our difficultness/sinfulness is the basis for how we are to respond to difficult people, which is with grace.

As believers in Christ our mandate is not to get even or return evil for evil but to return evil with good (Romans 12:19–21). We are called to love our enemies and to pray for those who persecute us (Matthew 5:43–45). This may seem impossible, and in our own power it is impossible. However, with God working in us it is possible (Matthew 19:26).

To return evil with good may chafe at our sense of justice, and sometimes rightly so. However, we must remember that it is God's role to mete out justice. We are to leave the matter in God's hands and trust that He will judge justly (Romans 12:19). Most importantly, we must realize that we have not received what we deserve from God but have received mercy and unmerited favour instead. While we were hostile and at enmity with God, He sent His Son to die for our sins (Romans 5:6–8; Ephesians 2:1– 10). Jesus, even while He was being persecuted, prayed for His tormentors (Luke 23:34).

As a point of clarity, it is not wrong to involve legal authorities. Criminal behaviour is not what we are referring to when we talk about "difficult people." Social authorities have been put in place by God to uphold the law, and it is not wrong to use them (Romans 13:1–7). However, we are not to seek societal justice out of vengeance. Similarly, depending on the difficult behaviour, it is not wrong to involve church authorities. Matthew 18:15–20 outlines the proper procedure for addressing grievances among church members. Again, the intent is not to seek vengeance, but to bring about peace.

As believers in Christ we are indwelt by the Spirit of God who produces the attitudes of love, joy, peace, longsuffering (patience, forbearance), kindness, goodness, faithfulness, gentleness, and self-control (Galatians 5:22–23). Therefore, we are to pray to be filled with the Spirit and to keep in step with the Spirit, and not grieve Him (Ephesians 4:30; 5:18; Galatians 5:25). If we are to respond to difficult people with grace and love, we must depend upon and draw upon the power of God's Spirit. When we become angry and return evil with evil, we must quickly confess our sin and ask God for the grace to imitate Jesus Christ and show ourselves to be sons and daughters of our merciful Father (Luke 6:36). If we refuse to love our enemies then we are imitating not our Heavenly Father, but the unforgiving servant (Matthew 18:21–35). It is in our eternal best interest to imitate the former and not the latter. How can we who have received such grace and forgiveness from God refuse to show the same to others?

Often it is simple to know how we should act toward difficult people, but it can be quite a challenge to do so in our daily lives. The Proverbs have some excellent practical advice. For example, Proverbs 15:1 says, "A soft answer turns away wrath, but a harsh word stirs up anger." We can memorize this verse and, when confronted by a difficult person, attempt to respond with gentleness. You might be surprised how the situation de-escalates. Proverbs 12:16 says, "The vexation of a fool is known at once, but the prudent ignores an insult." Rather than take insults personally and respond with immediate offense, we can learn to simply ignore them. Proverbs 20:3 says, "It is an honour for a man to keep aloof from strife, but every fool will be quarrelling." Titus 3:9 has similar encouragement to "avoid foolish controversies, genealogies, dissensions, and quarrels about the law, for they are unprofitable and worthless." Proverbs 17:14 similarly encourages ending quarrels before they begin. We can remind ourselves of the things that really matter and remember that some quarrels are simply pointless. There is no use getting entangled with a difficult person when the end result is "unprofitable and worthless."

In some situations, it is best to try to avoid certain difficult people altogether. Proverbs 22:24–25 says, "Make no friendship with a man given to anger, nor go with a wrathful man, lest you learn his ways and entangle yourself in a snare." First Corinthians 15:33 says, "Do not be deceived: 'Bad company ruins good morals.'" As much as we are able, we should make friendships with those who are seeking to honour God the same way we are. We are also called to live peaceably with others as far as we are able (Romans 12:18; Hebrews 12:14).

We can be proactive in dealing with difficult people by reading and even memorizing God's Word to give us the right perspective on life. His Word tells us that all people are made in His image (Genesis 1:26). When we view others as image-bearers, we may find it easier to bear with them. We can also recognize that dealing with difficult people is a trial that God can use to produce good things in us. For example, see how Romans 5:3–5 and James 1:2–5 address trials and hardships.

Dealing with difficult people becomes easier when we seek to exhibit empathy for others. We know that we ourselves can be difficult, particularly when tired or stressed or hungry. How would we want to be treated in such situations? Matthew 7:12 talks about doing unto others as we want them to do unto us. James 2:8 talks about loving others as we love ourselves. First Peter 4:8 says, "Above all, keep loving one another earnestly, since love covers a multitude of sins" (see also Proverbs 10:12). As we proactively seek to love one another, we will be more able to forgive offenses and deal with difficulties in a way that honours God.

Difficult people are often difficult as a result of their own pain. Seeing difficult people as those who are hurting and in need of Christ's touch can encourage us to forgive them. We can also pray for their healing. Perhaps in showing them kindness their hearts will be softened to Christ.

At times we will need to confront a difficult person or point out challenging inter- personal behaviours. This will hopefully help them stop inflicting damage on others around them as well as aid them in their own spiritual growth. Christians are called to speak truth in love (Ephesians 4:15). This means that we speak truth because we love and also do so from a heart of love. Truth can sometimes be hard to share and hard to receive, but we speak it with grace out of love for others. If the difficult person in our life is an unbeliever, we share the truth of the gospel with them as well.

Dealing with difficult people requires prayer and the power of God. When we know we are going to encounter a difficult person, we should pray beforehand. Ask for God's wisdom and His strength to respond well. Pray for the person and for God's work in his or her life. Remind yourself of some of the biblical truths shared here. Then seek to love as best as you can. Take any frustrations or emotional pain from your interaction with the difficult person straight to God and seek His healing and comfort.

DOES THE BIBLE SAY ANYTHING ABOUT LONELINESS?

It is both ironic and tragic that in a time where we are more connected technologically than ever, we also see some of the highest recorded rates of loneliness in history. Loneliness is not about being with people—we can feel lonely surrounded by others and not feel lonely when we are alone. Loneliness is an emotional state in which we feel isolated or completely alone in the world. And though it seems this emotional state is becoming more commonly chronic, loneliness itself is not a new phenomenon.

The first mention of loneliness is found in Genesis 2:18, where God states that it is not good that man should be alone. God's remedy for Adam's loneliness is the creation of Eve and the institution of marriage (Genesis 2:21–24). God provided Adam with a companion – a helpmate also made in the image of God – to join him in life. Throughout Scripture we see the importance of companionship, friendship, and fellowship. People were built for relationship—with both God and one another.

When Adam and Eve sinned, relationships broke down. Not only was humanity separated from God, human relationship was damaged (Genesis 3:16, 24). No longer did peace exist between humans and God or between humans and one another. However, even as God pronounced the consequences of Adam and Eve's sin, He also granted hope: the proto-evangelium (Genesis 3:15). This hope was the promise of a Saviour who would defeat Satan and restore peace between God and mankind. This Saviour is Jesus Christ, and He is the only true and lasting remedy for loneliness.

It is through Jesus that we are reconciled to God (2 Corinthians 5:18–21). Jesus is the one who has laid down His life for His friends (John 15:13–15). To paraphrase Pascal, "There is a God-shaped vacuum in every human heart." That vacuum manifests itself in the ache of restlessness and loneliness, which is only soothed by the peace and love of God found in Jesus Christ (John 14:27; Matthew 11:28–30). And what can separate us from the love of God in Christ? Nothing (Romans 8:35–39). To all who believe in Jesus, He has given the Holy Spirit to live inside us and be with us forever (John 14:15–17). He promises that He is with us always (Matthew 28:20). In Jesus, we are never isolated or alone.

It is also through God's work that we are reconciled to other people (Ephesians 2:11– 22). Having received the Spirit of God and the example of Christ, we learn to put pride aside and seek to meet the needs of others and not ourselves only (Philippians 2:3– 8). As husbands and wives grow in their love for and service to Jesus Christ, they learn to love and serve one another (Ephesians 5:22–25). Likewise, children learn loving submission to parents and parents learn not to exasperate their children (Ephesians 6:1–4). Although relationships are not perfect this side of heaven, they can be restored, established, and strengthened by the grace of God. Restored relationships functioning in mutual submission mean less loneliness.

Even more, in Christ, we have become part of a new spiritual family that is one hundred times larger than any natural family. Love of and loyalty to Christ can sometimes cause even our natural families to turn against us. However, God more than makes up for such losses, both in this world and in the world to come (Matthew 19:29). As believers in Christ, we have become part of the family of God and that is a big family. A family where no one need be lonely.

So, if you are feeling lonely ask yourself if you have been reconciled to God by believing in Jesus Christ. If you have, then remind yourself of the promise that God has made to you, "... I will never leave you nor forsake you" (Hebrews 13:5). Jesus, who died for you, has gone to prepare a place for you where you will dwell with Him and all who belong to Him eternally (John 14:1–3). In the meantime, He has given us His Spirit to dwell within us, teach us, and comfort us (John 14:16–18). No believer in Christ is ever truly alone.

WHO WAS LILLITH / LILITH? DID ADAM HAVE ANOTHER WIFE BEFORE EVE?

Lilith is a mythological character purported to have been Adam's first wife. The Bible contains no such account nor even hints at such a possibility. According to the legend, Lilith was headstrong and independent, and didn't want to submit to Adam, so she divorced him. How the Lilith legend came to be is a circuitous tale on its own.

The legend of Lilith originated in the last chapter of the Epic of Gilgamesh—a chapter which was probably not original to the rest of the text. In the story, the goddess Inanna finds a tree in a river and plants it in her garden. She cares for it for ten years, but finds that it's been infested with "the serpent who could not be charmed," "the Anzu-bird," and "the dark maid Lilith." Inanna cannot get rid of the squatters, so she asks her brother Gilgamesh. He strikes the serpent, leading the Anzu-bird to flee with its young and Lilith to smash her home and escape to "the wild, uninhabited places." Gilgamesh chops up the tree and makes a throne and a bed for Inanna.

The Aleppo National Museum is in possession of an amulet with the engraving of a sphinx and a she-wolf that includes the words "O, Demoness-that-flies in a dark chamber, Get on your way at once, O Lili!" The amulet is thought to be Syrian, from the 6th or 7th century BC, but it's also possible it's a forgery from the 1930s.

It's possible that the Bible references Lilith as a pagan character. Isaiah 34:14 reads, "And wild animals shall meet with hyenas; the wild goat shall cry to his fellow; indeed, there the night bird settles and finds for herself a resting place." The night bird (some translations say "screech owl") is the Hebrew Liyliyth. It is derived from layil, which means "night." "Lilith," literally, means "night maid," so it's unclear if the verse refers to the Sumerian goddess or if it's a poetic way to describe a female nocturnal bird.

Some argue for Lilith's existence by pointing to the seeming conflict between Genesis 1 and 2. In Genesis 1:27, God creates male and female. But Genesis 2:18–25 tells the story of the creation of Eve. In truth, Genesis 1 is a synopsis of the six days of creation while Genesis 2 gives more detail into the sixth day when God created Adam and Eve. But many people misinterpret the timeline and think the chapters are straight chronology. Genesis 1:27, they say, refers to Lilith.

Extra-biblical writings of Judaism hold to this account. The midrash Genesis Rabba (AD 300—500) infers that Adam had a first wife. The Babylonian Talmud says that Lilith has wings, that she can cause birth defects, that she is a succubus, and that she used the nocturnal emissions of sleeping men to conceive demon babies. The first text that clearly connects Lilith as Adam's first wife is The Alphabet of Ben Sira. In this text, Lilith is said to have left Adam when he demanded she be submissive in sex. When Adam asked angels to bring her back, she said she wouldn't. The angels told her they would kill her demon children, so she responded that she would in turn kill the babies of the descendants of Adam.

Further legend says that she is responsible for diphtheria, stillborn children, and babies who die of SIDS. It was a short leap to go from Lilith as "night maid" to "night hag," and blame her for sleep paralysis. Some, including Michelangelo, associate her with the serpent that tempted Eve. In this incarnation, she is the wife of Satan and provides the body so that he can be the voice that talks to Eve.

More recently, feminists and New Agers have claimed Lilith as a role model. They praise her independence and sexual freedom and use her as an example when refusing to submit to their husbands. She has leant her name to "Lilith Fair," a touring concert of female singers and female-led bands, and Lilith Magazine, a Jewish feminist magazine.

The only verified part of all this is that Lilith was a character in ancient Sumerian/Akkadian folk lore. Any "evidence" found in the Bible is easily dismissed. The bulk of literature defining her role in history comes from Kabbalah—a Jewish- based cult. In short, Lilith was a figure of ancient mythology who has since been used to represent death to innocents, sexual predation on men, and feminist independence. She was never real, and she certainly was never married to Adam.

DOES SEX EQUAL MARRIAGE? ARE UNMARRIED COUPLES WHO HAVE SEX MARRIED IN THE EYES OF GOD?

The short answer to the question of whether sex equals marriage is "no." Having sex does not make a couple married in God's eyes. Marriage is much more than just having one sex partner for the rest of your life; marriage is a total union of both persons physically, legally, and materially. To understand why having sex doesn't make a person married before God, one must understand how God views marriage and sex.

The Bible has many passages warning against sexual immorality, and fornication (sex before marriage) is included within this range of acts (Acts 15:20; 1 Corinthians 5:1; 6:13; Galatians 5:19; Ephesians 5:3; Colossians 3:5; 1 Thessalonians 4:3; Jude 1:7). Having sex with your significant other does not make you married because marriage is more than sex. Sex does not equal marriage. Marriage is the legally binding promise to give yourself wholly to another for the rest of your life. Sex before marriage is damaging because it separates sex from this promise. God, knowing the beauty and intimacy of sex, protects us from hurting ourselves when He tells us to reserve sex for marriage.

God created marriage as a covenant, and He is the one who binds the couple together (Matthew 19:6). Sex then becomes the act of that covenant by binding a man and woman together in physical and spiritual intimacy that mirrors the legal binding together of the couple (Genesis 2:24). Sex is a way of giving yourself completely to another person, and the covenant of marriage provides the freedom and safety to give oneself wholly (Matthew 19:6). This is a great promise, and because of that Paul writes that we should "Let marriage be held in honour among all, and let the marriage bed be undefiled" (Hebrews 13:4).

You may be unmarried and having sex with your partner with the full intention of loving them for the rest of your life. If so, what is stopping you from making this promise before God and before the law through marriage? Sex without marriage holds on to the option of walking away when one's needs are not being met, but this is not the covenantal love of marriage. This is love that keeps oneself first rather than one's significant other. God's desire is for us to enjoy all the love and support of intimate, committed relationships, and therefore He has given us the best way we can experience this on earth through marriage.

WILL MARRIAGE EXIST IN HEAVEN?

Matthew 22:30 provides a clear answer to the question of whether there will be marriage in heaven. Jesus stated, "For in the resurrection they neither marry nor are given in marriage, but are like angels in heaven." Jesus personally stated that marriage would not exist in heaven.

Many have speculated as to why marriage will not exist in heaven. The Bible does not directly address these reasons, but says we will be like the angels in heaven (v. 30b). What does this mean? Angels are called "ministering spirits" in Hebrews 1:14 who are "sent out to serve for the sake of those who are to inherit salvation." In other words, at least one way human life will be different in heaven is that our lives will be completely focused on worship and service of God.

Second, it is clear that in heaven God will provide complete contentment and satisfaction. As part of His perfect, eternal plan, marriage will no longer be necessary in heaven. All redeemed people will live as brothers and sisters in Christ in perfect harmony. Revelation 21:4 clearly notes this perfect situation: "He will wipe away every tear from their eyes, and death shall be no more, neither shall there be mourning, nor crying, nor pain anymore, for the former things have passed away."

Third, the discontinuation of marriage in heaven will remove all problems associated with marriages on earth consisting of one believer and one unbeliever. This would otherwise cause many complications and create several other questions that would need to be solved.

Fourth, the focus in heaven will not be on creating and building a family but rather on enjoying the family of God already designed in heaven. There will be no need to build families through marriage or raising children. No one will ever die again and life will extend throughout a perfect, sinless eternity.

Finally, some have noted that marriage originally arose out of need for a "suitable helper" for Adam in Genesis 2:18 when he had no one else to live with in family and community. In heaven, this need for community will no longer exist as male and female will dwell in perfect community with the Lord and all believers for all time.

Should the end of marriage in heaven be a concern to us? By no means! When the apostle John saw what would take place at the end of time, he was not discouraged. Instead, he responded, "Amen. Come, Lord Jesus!" (Revelation 22:20). He knew that eternity future would be far greater than any human relationship or family in this life.

DOES THE BIBLE SAY ANYTHING ABOUT INTERRACIAL MARRIAGE?

Both the Bible and science concur: there is no such thing as interracial marriage. The subdivisions of mankind that we refer to as "races" do not genetically exist. There is exactly one race of human beings. There are ethnic and cultural differences, but the biological differences are so slight that they cannot be said to represent a different life form.

In spiritual terms, there are two races of humans: Jesus-followers and everyone else; those with a heart of stone, and those with a heart of flesh (Ezekiel 11:19). Second Corinthians 6:14 prohibits Christians from marrying non-Christians. This law was paralleled in Israel in the Old

Testament (Deuteronomy 7:3-4) which forbade the Israelites from marrying foreigners of a different religion. But there are many marriages and children of mixed ethnicity that are held up with honour. Caleb's father is called a Kenizzite (Numbers 32:12)—descended from one of the nations of Canaan. Rahab was from Jericho (Joshua 2). Moses' wife was a Cushite from Midian (Exodus 2:16-21)—as was her father who served as a counsellor for Moses (Exodus 18:17-27). Ruth the Moabitess has an entire book dedicated to her and her faithfulness to her Jewish mother-in-law. In the New Testament, Timothy was the son of a Jewish mother and a Greek father, and a leader in the early church.

There seems to be a general pattern among interethnic marriages in societies. A group of men, whether explorers, traders, job-hunters, or refugees, will enter another country. They will intermarry with local women, to varying degrees. Such marriages will be socially acceptable until the arrival of one or more factors: fear that the local culture will become diluted, the introduction of slavery of others of the men's nationality, or possibly the introduction of women of the ethnic minority. Sex slavery of girls and women generally leads to a great amount of interethnic marriages, as does the combination of war with refugees. When native men are killed in war and refugees from that war immigrate in, interethnic marriages become common.

Barring the outside influence of foolish prejudice, native culture is a much bigger issue in relationships than skin colour. A couple's ancestry does not matter as much as the individual's family upbringing. When things such as conflict resolution and expectations differ greatly, ethnicity takes a back seat—and such issues can certainly strain a marriage between two people of the same ethnic background.

There are both advantages and disadvantages to mixed-ethnic relationships. Family and culture may prove to be difficult. But the more interethnic marriages a society witnesses, the more normalized they become. And it has been hypothesized that children of mixed parentage may have genetic benefits as damaging recessive genes are minimized.

There is nothing unbiblical about interethnic relationships. In fact, when Miriam challenged her brother Moses' authority by criticizing his mixed-ethnic marriage, God not only backed Moses and Zipporah, He gave Miriam leprosy for her disloyalty (Numbers 12). As God told Samuel, "… the Lord sees not as man sees: man looks on the outward appearance, but the Lord looks on the heart" (1 Samuel 16:7).

WHAT IS A BIBLICAL PERSPECTIVE ON MARITAL/SPOUSAL RAPE?

Marital rape occurs when one spouse forces the other to engage in unwanted sexual activity. It is non-consensual penetrative sex (vaginal, oral, anal) occurring within a marriage relationship. Most often the non-consenting partner is forced through violence or threats of violence, although other forms of coercion may be used. Sometimes the rape will be presented as "make-up sex" following a physical or verbal altercation. While not always the case, it seems that marital rape is more likely to be a pattern within a marriage than a one-time occurrence. It is also likely that other forms of domestic violence are present in the relationship.

The legal acknowledgement of spousal rape is relatively new. Some countries still do not recognize the possibility for rape within marriage. Historically, sex has been seen as something husbands always desire and to which wives must always submit. Others have believed that marriage is implicit consent to sex at any time. While some countries criminalized marital rape earlier than 1970, most Western countries did not discuss marital rape in their laws until the 1980s and 1990s. The exact definitions and provisions vary; some removed clauses that would restrict rape to an extramarital offense whereas others distinguish marital rape as a separate crime.

Victims of spousal rape face unique challenges. Emotionally and psychologically, rape within a marriage is received differently from stranger or even acquaintance rape. Sex is meant to be a unifying and beautiful event in marriage, not a venue for violence and coercion. Because of the intimacy of the marriage relationship, wounds from spousal rape can be broader than wounds from a more distant relationship.

Some have used passages like 1 Corinthians 7:1-5 and

Ephesians 5:22 to claim that the Bible does not recognize marital rape and that wives must always consent to sex. Using these passages in that way is a gross misinterpretation and misuse of the Word of God. Ephesians 5 discusses mutual submission built on a foundation of love and respect. It compares the relationship between husband and wife to that between Christ and the Church. Jesus never forces the Church to submit to His desires – let alone use violence. Rather, He willingly sacrificed Himself to save us and lovingly beckons believers to obedience for our own benefit (Mark 10:43-45; John 10:18; John 15:1-17; Philippians 2:3-11; 1 John 3:16-18). Rape is a selfish and violent act; Jesus Christ is neither selfish nor violent.

First Corinthians 7:1-5 also talks about mutuality. Verses 3-5 say, "The husband should give to his wife her conjugal rights, and likewise the wife to her husband. For the wife does not have authority over her own body, but the husband does. Likewise the husband does not have authority over his own body, but the wife does. Do not deprive one another, except perhaps by agreement for a limited time, that you may devote yourselves to prayer; but then come together again, so that Satan may not tempt you because of your lack of self-control." Paul clearly states that both husband and wife should give the other their sexual rights. Neither husband nor wife should deprive the other sexually. He clearly states that the wife's body belongs to the husband and also that the husband's body belongs to the wife – but that this is a willing giving of themselves, never a taking, which rape always is. One does not rule over the other; both husband and wife are given the same instructions and are expected to come to a place of agreement on sexual matters.

Sex is meant to be an expression of the oneness that is marriage (Genesis 2:24; Matthew 19:5; 1 Corinthians 6:16). Marriage is upheld as a unique institution that is not only foundational to society but images Christ and the Church. Violence of any kind has no place in a marriage. Sexual violence is especially damaging because it confounds the very core of the marriage bond.

If anyone has made sexual contact with you without your consent, please seek help. If you are currently in danger of being forced to have sex, or if forced sex is an established pattern between you and another person, call the police and get out of the situation as soon as it is safe for you to do so. There is absolutely nothing wrong with calling the police against a spouse or partner—rape is a felony and should be handled by law enforcement.

In addition to practical matters of removing oneself from the situation, receiving any medical care necessary, and potentially taking legal action, other recovery is needed. Victims of marital rape will very likely require counselling. The emotional and psychological implications of spousal rape can have long-lasting effects. The abused/ raped spouse should not feel pressured to return to the abuser without first receiving extensive input and counsel from licensed counsellors, government authorities, and trustworthy friends who understand the situation. Spiritually, victims may doubt God's goodness and His trustworthiness. Learning to feel safe with God, coming to believe that He is loving and gentle, and coming to trust Him will take time. He is willing and able to bring healing and forgiveness. Do not be afraid to take that time, or to walk beside someone who is asking hard questions about their faith.

Perpetrators of marital rape will need to come to recognize their own sin, repent, and get the help they need. Reasons a person might commit spousal rape are varied. In God, there is healing for past hurts, forgiveness for sins, and hope for a new future.

IS THE CONCEPT OF SOULMATES BIBLICAL?

The idea that God has designated a specific spouse for each person, or that everyone has a "soulmate" who is a "perfect fit" and apart from whom you can never be happy, is not biblical.

Sometimes, the idea of a soulmate confuses and delays a single person from committing to marriage. Sometimes, the idea of a soulmate provides an excuse to someone who is married to seek divorce. Both views are flawed.

Marriage is designed as a lifelong covenant, so it is wise not to enter into it lightly. But fear that we might be missing our true soulmate should not hinder moving forward with a

God-honouring relationship. Studying what the Bible says about marriage, praying over the decision, and getting wise counsel from those who know you well and also those with marriage experience are important things to do before getting married. But looking for someone who will "complete you" or be a "perfect fit" is largely fruitless. No human is meant to "complete" any other human. Only God can meet our deepest needs and speak to the most vacuous voids in our hearts. A spouse should certainly complement us and be a good fit. And clearly we do not want to marry someone for whom we do not have genuine love and affection. Marriage is meant to be a joyous and fruitful bond in which the spouses are better together than apart. But such a relationship is often not what is thought of when people refer to soulmates.

As stated above, marriage is a lifelong covenant. When we are married, our spouse is functionally our soulmate. In talking with the Pharisees about divorce laws, Jesus said, "… Because of your hardness of heart [Moses] wrote you this commandment. But from the beginning of creation, 'God made them male and female.' 'Therefore a man shall leave his father and mother and hold fast to his wife, and the two shall become one flesh.' So they are no longer two but one flesh. What therefore God has joined together, let not man separate" (Mark 10:5–9). Marriage joins a man and woman together. Being one flesh in marriage is what makes a person our soulmate.

This is not to say that people do not sometimes make unwise choices in a marriage partner. But the argument that we married the wrong person is not a biblical grounds for divorce. God is able to redeem even the hardest of marriages. The God who saves sinners from eternal damnation also transforms us (2 Corinthians 5:17–21; Philippians 1:6).

Both the single person and the married person should learn what the Bible says about marriage. Some places to start are Genesis 1—2, Ephesians 5:22–33, and Colossians 3:18–21.

When we trust in Him and not our own understanding, He will provide direction (Proverbs 3:5–6). When we continue growing our relationship with God, He will not fail to offer us direction and guidance in all areas of our life—including finding a spouse and throughout marriage. Sometimes God's direction comes through other people. So if confusion or doubt about your relationships remains, please seek out a pastor or Christian counsellor.

HOW RELIABLE WAS THE VIRGINITY TEST MENTIONED IN DEUTERONOMY 22?

Deuteronomy 22:13–21 is one of the most controversial passages in the Bible. The scenario is that of a man who has married a woman, consummates the marriage, and then complains to the village elders that she was not a virgin. Her parents bring proof of her virginity, and the man is found out.

For his offense, the accuser will be punished and fined. According to Josephus, the word translated "whip" in the ESV, "chastise" in the NASB, and "punish" in the NIV (Deuteronomy 22:18) refers to flogging—"forty stripes save one." The man is prohibited from ever divorcing the woman, which means her children have the right of inheritance (see Deuteronomy 21:15–17). And he is required to pay the woman's father one hundred shekels of silver for dishonouring his reputation. Consider that Joseph was sold to slavers for twenty silver shekels (Genesis 37:28) and this is twice the dowry of a woman who has been seduced or raped (Deuteronomy 22:29).

There are several issues that this law addresses.

> The woman is protected. In the culture of the Old Testament, women had almost no rights. If a man married a woman, had sex with her, and then claimed she was not a virgin, she would be divorced, dishonoured, and basically unmarriable – if the community didn't just stone her. Her options would be very limited, and her security would depend on a male relative having the mercy to support her. As in other places in the Mosaic Law, God protects the vulnerable. Not only is her honour restored, her future is established since the man is not allowed to divorce her in the future.

> God's plan for marriage is defended. In these times, marriage was usually not about romance. It

was a business contract between two families. The reason given for the groom's rejection is that he "hates" the woman, but he would not go to such lengths if he did not also revile her father. The entire purpose of marriage is disregarded, and the man uses the woman to dishonour her family. God did not create marriage as a business transaction, but as a relationship where two become one (Genesis 2:24).

> The honour of the bride's family is restored. The reason the woman's parents bring the evidence of her virginity (thought to be a sheet or garment with blood on it, the result of the consummation of the marriage) is because they presented her to the man as an eligible bride. With the evidence, the family is vindicated, and the man is revealed as a crook.

> The criminal is brought to justice. A few things need to happen before the groom makes the accusation. The man needs to hate the woman, or be ambivalent toward her but hate her father. He needs to feel so passionately that he would rather see her dead than just divorce her or marry a second wife. And he has to be a fool because he didn't look to see if she used a cloth to clean up. The punishment of the man reflects what his victims would have paid had the charge been true. The bride's family would have been dishonoured; the public flogging dishonours the man. The bride's father would have had to return the dowry;

the man has to pay yet more. The man would have been rid of the woman; now he can never send her away.

> Israel is sanctified. The entire situation acts as prevention for all sides. Men are warned not to bear false witness against their brides — or to marry women whose father they don't respect. Women are warned against promiscuity. And fathers are reminded that their daughters are not negotiating tools. Further, Israel is forewarned to remain faithful to God and not seek after foreign idols — a warning they will regularly ignore.

If the charge is true, however, and the woman and/or her father lied about her virginity, she is to be stoned at her father's doorstep. Her punishment is rather obvious; she deceitfully presented herself to the groom as a virgin. The location of the stoning reflects on her father's honour. If the father used his daughter in another business deal (remember how Saul gave his daughter Michal to David, and then, after David left, to Palti in 1 Samuel 25:44), the father deserves the public dishonour. If the woman had sex without her father's knowledge, the dishonour is that he didn't control his child. It's been suggested that stoning was the ultimate punishment out of many options, and the groom could have chosen something less extreme, as Joseph intended with Mary (Matthew 1:19).

The inherent ambiguities in the law led to some interesting traditions and notes in the halakhah (the Jewish religious laws collected from the Written and Oral Torah).

Sometimes the bride and groom were searched before consummating the marriage — she for a pre-stained cloth and he for a clean one. Groomsmen would enter into the bed chamber afterward to find the cloth and make sure the groom hadn't hidden it. If a woman was suspected of promiscuity before the wedding, she would be inspected by "reliable, honest women." Although their examination couldn't have been absolute, they were experienced, and their judgment would have been more accurate than a cloth. In one case, in the sixteenth or seventeenth century, a three-year old girl who fell from a chair was examined by such women who gave her parents a certificate stating the girl's hymen was not broken by intercourse.

The law was radical for its time in its protection of women, but there are three major controversies that this passage brings up today. The first is, why was there a test for the bride and not the groom? Why the emphasis on a woman's virginity and not a man's? This argument doesn't take into account the historical and cultural context of the law. At this time and place, men had all the power. Women had none. It was a sin for a man to have sex outside of marriage, but in the culture, he was rarely seriously punished for it unless he slept with another's wife (Deuteronomy 22:22). Changing this culture would have required changing the hearts of all involved, which would have been very difficult without the indwelling of the Holy Spirit and submission to His leading. So, as God did frequently with His laws regarding women and slaves, He established protection for the vulnerable in the context of men's business dealings.

The second controversy is, what if the woman had no proof? What if her hymen was broken already? What if she just didn't bleed? There have been many speculative answers to this question. Girls didn't do gymnastics or ride bikes, so they wouldn't have broken yet. Sex was rough, not the gentle love-making we think of, and so there would have been damage. Girls were probably married shortly after puberty; they would have been small, and again the rough sex with a full-grown man would have caused damage. The facts of the matter are, the law gave protection where previously there had been none, and the process allowed intervention by God. It's possible that He could have caused the girl to bleed to protect her, even if she wouldn't have naturally.

There is also some discussion as to the exact wording of Deuteronomy 22:20. It's been suggested that the clauses "if the thing is true" and "evidence of virginity was not found" are not directly connected. So even if the cloth was absent, the groom would still have to find incontrovertible proof, such as a confession or witnesses.

The final question is, why the harsh punishment? How is stoning a just consequence for not being a virgin? This is not the only sin that is held in such serious regard. For example, enticing someone to worship an idol (Deuteronomy 13:1–11); blasphemy (Leviticus 24:11–16); working on the Sabbath (Numbers 15:32–36); rebelling against one's parents (Deuteronomy 21:18–21); premeditated murder (Exodus 21:12–14); adultery, homosexual sex, and bestiality (Leviticus 20:10–16); kidnapping (Exodus 21:16); and lying in an investigation

(Deuteronomy 19:15–21) were all capital offenses. They were also all related to one of the Ten Commandments.

Deuteronomy 22:21 explains why: "… you shall purge the evil from your midst." God's chosen people are to live differently than those around them. We are often quick to criticize the severity of God's punishments in the Mosaic Law. But that criticism doesn't reveal God's cruelty, it reveals our too-easy acceptance of sin (1 Peter 1:16).

There is no passage in the Bible that describes a bride being stoned after her groom found or suspected she was not a virgin. Despite the seeming unfairness of the law, it's important to remember that God's law does not validate abusing the vulnerable, it reveals our natural tendency to do so.

WHAT GROUNDS FOR DIVORCE DOES THE BIBLE PROVIDE?

The grounds for divorce given in the Bible sound constricting to modern ears. The teachings on divorce address the issues of the day, which were very different than modern times. Add to that some seemingly contradictory passages and confusing turns of phrase, and things get even muddier.

When God first created the marriage relationship, divorce was not a part of the plan. Fallen man, as he often does, defiled God's intent for His creation. When the Pharisees asked Jesus if a man could divorce his wife at will, Jesus responded:

He answered, "Have you not read that he who created them from the beginning made them male and female, and said, 'Therefore a man shall leave his father and his mother and hold fast to his wife, and the two shall become one flesh'? So they are no longer two but one flesh. What therefore God has joined together, let not man separate" (Matthew 19:4-6)

When asked about grounds for divorce in the time of Moses, Jesus said, "Moses permitted you to divorce your wives because your hearts were hard. But it was not this way from the beginning. I tell you that anyone who divorces his wife, except for sexual immorality, and marries another woman commits adultery" (Matthew 19:8-9). In the Old Testament, God allowed divorce if a man's heart became so hardened against his wife that she was actually better off without him—a rare and extreme circumstance in a time where women had very few legal rights. This was the purpose of the dowry— presumably the husband had set aside money at the beginning of their marriage to see to his bride's needs should he abandon her by death or divorce.

As Jesus mentioned, this was not God's intent for marriage. Marriage was to be a permanent illustration of God's love and devotion to Israel. If a man was cruel or abusive to his wife, he was not reflecting the kind, forgiving spirit of God. A man who divorced his wife under such circumstances was not to marry again; God was faithful to the "wife of His youth" despite Israel's spiritual adultery (Malachi 2:14), and a man who couldn't love his wife as God loved Israel was not worthy of getting a new wife. As Malachi 2:16 (NIV) says, "The man who hates and divorces his wife…does violence to the one he should protect."

Taken in the whole, a man was not to divorce his wife unless she was unfaithful, or he was abusive and the divorce was protection for the wife. If the divorce was not because of unfaithfulness on her part, he was not allowed to remarry (Matthew 19:9).

These were the grounds for divorce for Israel, but the church age is slightly different. A wife had few people to protect her from her husband in the Old Testament; a wife in the latter New Testament and beyond has the church. Matthew 18:15-17 describes the steps of reconciliation Christians should take in their relationships and dealings with others: confront privately, seek counselling, and take it to the church.

First Corinthians 7:10-16 describes grounds for divorce for believers. First of all, believing spouses are assumed to be led by the Holy Spirit, not their own selfish desires. Believers are supposed to work with the Spirit in the process of sanctification, growing from glory to glory as they strive to be more like Christ. This, combined with Matthew 18:15-17, should resolve any issue that would otherwise lead to divorce. If both spouses are humble and patient and kind and loving, and live with a healthy, supportive church, they should have the tools to successfully wade through any issue.

First Corinthians 7:10-11 allows that this doesn't always happen. Those who are immature in the faith may not have the spiritual tools to weather difficult marriages. Paul is clear: marriage is an illustration of God's relationship with the church (Ephesians 5:32). That relationship is supposed to be faithful and permanent. Divorce and remarriage is not appropriate for personal difficulties. Although it is certainly not ideal, separation with the goal of reconciliation is allowed.

The Bible also describes grounds for divorce if one spouse is a believer but the other is not. Ideally, it is better for them to remain together. The godly influence of the Christian spouse will bring peace and blessing to the family that would be removed if the marriage were dissolved. The non-Christian will be subtly influenced by the loving behaviour of the believing spouse. But if the unbelieving spouse leaves, the Christian is required to let him go. In modern times, this means that if the unbelieving spouse files for divorce, the Christian must sign the paperwork.

Not all believers live out their faith. Often, one spouse will be closer to the Lord than the other. First Corinthians 7:12-16 addresses this situation as well. The last statement in the steps of resolution Jesus gives in Matthew 18:15-17 says that if every avenue has tried and failed, the sinner is to be considered as "a Gentile and a tax collector"— that is, as an unbeliever. If it comes to this, the same rules apply: if steps of reconciliation have been followed but one believing spouse still files for divorce, the other must sign.

These passages describe the biblical grounds for divorce: adultery and abandonment. Adultery because it defiles God's use of marriage to represent His love for Israel and the church. Abandonment because we are called to live in peace. This can be very hard to swallow for those who feel they are trapped in a loveless marriage. But our relationship with God is to be above our relationship with others. Our personal and corporate commandment is "love God, love others." There is no better way to love others than to do what we can to draw them to God. Sometimes we need a break, and sometimes a partner can completely destroy any chance we have to reach them. But through any situation, God can lead us through a way in which we will not sin—which is faithfulness to Him (1 Corinthians 10:13).

WHAT DOES IT MEAN TO LEAVE AND CLEAVE?

"Leave and cleave" comes from Genesis 2:24. After God created Eve and Adam declared that she was "bone of my bones and flesh of my flesh" (Genesis 2:23), Genesis says, "Therefore a man shall leave his father and his mother and hold fast to his wife, and they shall become one flesh" (Genesis 2:24). The ESV translates "cleave" as "hold fast." Some translations, such as the KJV, use the word "cleave," others say "is united" (NIV), or "be joined" (NASB).

This cleaving is further described as "become one flesh"—an intimate cohesion that includes, but means more than, the physical union. Cleave and becoming one flesh is an intimate, soul-level adherence to one another that God intended for two people in a committed marriage. This joining is meant to be permanent, last through the tough times, look out for the interests of the other, and move as one.

Both the husband and wife are called to leave and cleave. Their allegiance is no longer primarily to the family they were born into, but to their spouse. This does not mean a person has to turn away from their parents, but give their new family, beginning with their spouse, pre-eminence. This builds cohesion and intimacy and oneness.

God calls those in marriage to act and reflect His own relationship with the church (Ephesians 5). Husbands and wives are to honour and serve one another. This relationship is meant to be the most fulfilling, emotionally and physically, connection one person has with another human being—for a lifetime.

HOW CAN A CHRISTIAN 'LEAVE AND CLEAVE' AND STILL HONOR THEIR PARENTS?

The Bible tells us that when we marry, we are to leave our parents and cleave to our spouse (Genesis 2:24). At the same time, the Bible instructs us to honour our parents (Exodus 20:12, Ephesians 6:1–3) and care for them when they need help (1 Timothy 5:3–8).

Marriage relationships are intended to be lifelong and to take precedence over our relationship with our parents. In marriage, the two become "one flesh" (Genesis 2:24; Matthew 19:6). The husband and wife relationship is primary. We "leave" our parents and "cleave" to our spouse, thus forming a new family. At the same time, we still honour our parents.

At times it can feel like a parent is pulling a child away from a marriage, or like a marriage is restricting a child from honouring and caring for parents. Understanding what God's Word says about each relationship helps us know how to navigate when there are potential conflicts.

As has been stated, marriage is a lifelong commitment in which two people become one. There should be, between husband and wife, a growing oneness in every aspect of your life: emotional, intellectual, financial, physical, social, and familial. When an overbearing parent threatens this bond, appropriate boundaries need to be put in place. We are still respectful toward parents, but we do not allow the parent-child relationship to become primary. We are intended to "leave" the parent-child relationship.

At the same time, when our parent has a legitimate need, even if our spouse does not like our parent, we are to meet the need (Mark 7:10–13; 1 Timothy 5:4–8). When both husband and wife are seeking to honour God, even if the circumstance is uncomfortable, it is possible to honour both sets of parents and care for their needs while still keeping the marriage bond primary.

This balance can be compared to another in Scripture, that of obeying those in authority (Romans 13). We are instructed to honour those in authority, but the Bible also gives examples when apostles defied authorities to continue preaching the gospel (Acts 4:1–22). Each and every human relationship must submit to our relationship with God Himself (Luke 14:26). If a parent seeks to violate our marriage relationship, we reject that. If a spouse seeks to violate the call to honour parents, we reject that. We are to do all of this with respect and in submission to God.

We will need God's wisdom to discern what true needs are and what is overbearing, manipulative, or dishonouring. We should discuss these matters with our spouses and our parents as well. When all parties involved are seeking to honour God, things go much more smoothly. At the very least, when expectations are made clear, there is less risk of hurt feelings or confusion. As in all things, seek God's wisdom (James 1:5) in balancing the need to leave your parents and cleave to your spouse with the call to honour your parents.

WHAT DOES THE BIBLE SAY ABOUT HAVING A MARITAL/SEXUAL RELATIONSHIP WITH A CLOSE RELATIVE?

There are two reasons why we should not have a sexual/marital relationship with a close relative. The scientific reason is the threat of congenital defects in the offspring, and is often enforced by civil law. The biblical reason has more to do with the health of the extended family. While laws usually do not address this aspect, we should still consider the wisdom of considering the bigger picture.

When God made Adam and Eve in the Garden of Eden, they were genetically perfect. They had no congenital defects, no diseases lurking in their DNA. Such issues came into the human race gradually, over the course of several thousand years. It's possible that the environmental changes after the Flood had a part in accelerating cell damage; perhaps people were exposed to more cosmic and solar radiation as the drastic decrease in ages after the Flood suggests. Adam and Eve's children married their full- siblings. Two thousand years later, Abraham was Sarah's half-brother. There were many marriages between cousins in the Old Testament, including those of Isaac, Esau, and Jacob. In fact, marriage between first cousins is still allowed in some states in the U.S. And a study in the Journal of Genetic Counselling in 2002 showed that children of first-cousins have only about a 2-3% higher risk of birth defects than normal—a number comparable to the defects in a child born of a 41-year-old woman as opposed to 30 years of age.

Over the course of history, societies have progressively banned marriages and sexual relations between descendants (father/daughter; grandmother/grandson; etc.) and siblings because of genetic issues with more direct inbreeding. The bans were made easier to accommodate with the invention of the bicycle and then the car—suitors were able to go farther distances to find potential mates. These taboos tend to be enforced by law. (It could be argued that Genesis 2:24 indicates that marriage between children and parents was never allowed by God).

Although science gives a powerful motivation to avoid marriage among close relations, the Bible's laws on incest do not address genetic anomalies or congenital defects. The laws in Leviticus 18 suggest another motivation. These are the relationships God forbade to intermarry: Mother/stepmother and son (vs. 7-8) Sister/half-sister and brother (vs. 9, 11) Grandchild and grandparent (vs. 10) Aunt and nephew (vs. 12)

A man and his uncle's wife (v.14) Daughter-in-law and father-in-law (vs. 15) Sister-in-law and brother-in-law (vs. 16)

A woman and her daughter and the same man (vs. 17)

A woman and her granddaughter and the same man (vs. 17) A woman and her sister and the same man (vs. 18)

The reasons for the restrictions seem to be relational, not health-based. It was disrespectful to "uncover the nakedness" of one's parent or child, to include having sex with those relations' spouses. To have sex with a step-mother, aunt, daughter-in- law, or sibling was to upset the delicate balance of relationships in the family. It was dishonouring to the participants and their spouses. The two exceptions were if a man's wife died, he could marry her sister (vs. 18), and if a man died childless, his brother was expected to marry the widow and provide an heir. In either case, relational rivalry wouldn't be an issue.

The decision to marry a close relative, then, becomes a matter of three different factors. Is it legal? Different states and countries have different laws regarding marriage between relatives. Does it endanger the health of the children? Some states require marriages between first cousins to be sterile. Would the relationship be disrespectful to anyone involved to the point that it affects the peace of the extended family? If those issues are clear, there is nothing biblical against marriage between close relatives, and it becomes a matter of prayer and wisdom.

DOES THE BIBLE SAY ANYTHING ABOUT SEX ADDICTION?

A sex addiction is usually defined as frequent pursuit of sexual activity, despite knowing that negative consequences are occurring (or can occur) because of it. It has been categorized like other addictions, such as alcoholism or drug addiction.

Without question, there are addictive aspects associated with one's pursuit of sexual activity. At the same time, the Bible speaks about sexual activity as more than a mere "addiction." Within the confines of marriage, sex is an expression of love and a means of unity. It is a gift of God given for the enjoyment of each spouse, the strengthening of the marital bond, and procreation. Sex within a marriage is not meant as a means of pleasing oneself, but as a way of expressing love to one's spouse. So even within marriage a sex "addiction," in the sense of pursuing sex for the sake of sex and regardless of negative consequences, has no place; a spouse is not merely an avenue to fulfil sexual urges, but a committed partner for life. Perhaps more often, sex addiction is spoken of outside the confines of heterosexual marriage. The Bible calls all sexual behaviour outside of marriage between a man and woman sinful (Acts 15:20; 1 Corinthians 5:1; 6:13; Ephesians 5:3; Hebrews 13:4). Regardless of a person's inclinations or desires, following through on those desires in ungodly ways is sinful, whether with an addictive mentality or not.

It's important to distinguish between normal, healthy sexual desires and "sex addiction." God designed us to experience sexual pleasure. He specifically made men and women to attract each other, and to physically complement each other. Sexual desires are as natural as the desire to eat, breathe, and sleep. As with all of those, however, there are proper and improper ways to respond to natural urges. Even the things God made for our good can become a problem when we abuse them.

In addition to physical sexual immorality, the Bible further notes that the lusts involved in one's sexual desires can be sinful. Jesus said, "You have heard that it was said, 'You shall not commit adultery.' But I say to you that everyone who looks at a woman with lustful intent has already committed adultery with her in his heart" (Matthew 5:27–28). This includes pornography, sexual fantasies, and unhealthy flirting or interactions with others.

Thankfully, the Bible also offers hope for a new way of life. Many people who have considered themselves addicted to sex have found a new way of life through Jesus Christ. He provides forgiveness of sins (1 John 1:8–9), power to resist temptation (1 Corinthians 10:13), and new habits to replace our old sinful habits (Galatians 5:22– 23). Further, Christians have the wisdom of God's Word (2 Timothy 3:16–17), the power of prayer, and the help of other believers to encourage in holy living (Hebrews 10:25).

What can a person do who desires to overcome sexual addiction? First, it is important to become a believer in Jesus Christ if you have not already done so. For believers in Christ, you can confess your sins, knowing you will be forgiven (1 John 1:8–9). Trying to overcome addiction without the influence of the Holy Spirit is not only difficult, it is nearly impossible.

Second, replace your "old habits" with new, godly habits. Instead of spending time thinking about sexual thoughts, replace these thoughts with Christian music, Scripture memory, or investing your time to serve others in need. Be careful to recognize the situations that lead to sexual temptation. Addictions become much easier to overcome when you give yourself "breathing room" to get your mind right (Romans 12:2). Knowing where and when sexually tempting thoughts tend to occur gives you a way to avoid them entirely; this makes you far stronger and more prepared when they catch you off-guard.

Third, find a healthy friend or community of friends to help. The Christian life is not intended as a solo sport. Instead, regularly spend time with others where you can encourage one another, pray for one another, and provide accountability for areas of weakness (Galatians 6:1; Proverbs 27:17). When someone you love and trust is watching your back, it not only keeps you on track, it gives you somewhere to turn when you're feeling weak or vulnerable.

Fourth, God's recommendation for those who struggle with sexual desires is to marry. First Corinthians 7:2 teaches, "But because of the temptation to sexual immorality, each man should have his own wife and each woman her own husband." God gave us hunger, and good food. He gave us thirst, and water. He also gave us sexuality, and within the context of Christian marriage, believers can enjoy sexual intimacy in the way God intended. This is a powerful remedy to certain aspects of sexual addiction, since it gives us a legitimate means to express sexual desires. However, marriage in and of itself does not cure sexual addition, nor does it help with all sexual sins. In fact, some sex addictions, such as pornography or adultery, can destroy a marriage.

Sexual sin is one of the most difficult to overcome in the modern world. Imagine a culture where every street corner, TV ad, and movie was saturated in cocaine, heroin, and other drugs. A world where seemingly everyone at work was casual—even bragging—about their use of these drugs. Imagine a culture where using these substances was not only considered normal, but those who chose not to participate were treated as strange. Sadly, especially in the West, this is the attitude taken towards sex. It is a pervasive, invasive, intrusive part of the culture.

What's critical to remember is that sexual sin is fundamentally just like any other. God despises all sin, but He loves the people caught up in them. He loves sinners enough to die for them (Philippians 2:5–8), forgive them (1 John 2:1), and heal them (1 Corinthians 6:9–11). If you or someone you love is struggling with sexual addiction, there are powerful resources available to help you. None is more powerful than the God who knows what it means to suffer human temptation (Hebrews 4:15).

WHAT ARE SOME OF THE PARALLELS BETWEEN JEWISH WEDDING TRADITIONS AND OUR RELATIONSHIP TO CHRIST?

In the Old Testament, God often refers to His relationship with His chosen people in terms of a marriage where He is the husband and His people are the wife (Isaiah 54:5; Jeremiah 31:32; Hosea 2:16). Jesus continues this metaphor in the New Testament (Matthew 9:15; 25:1–13). And Paul refers to Christ as the husband to the believing church in 2 Corinthians 11:2 and Ephesians 5:25–27. In Revelation 19:7 and 21:9, God gives John a vision of a wedding feast at the end of time. So to fully understand the metaphor God employs throughout the Bible, one should investigate Jewish wedding traditions.

The first thing to note is that there are two stages to a traditional Jewish wedding. The first stage is the kiddushin, or betrothal period, when the couple are set apart from others and become dedicated exclusively to one another (sanctification). This is a period of intention and preparation. The husband would offer a bride price to the woman's family to make his intentions known. When those intentions were agreed to and the bride price paid and accepted, he would then prepare a home for him and his wife to live in after the wedding ceremony. The woman would be collecting her dowry to bring into the marriage with her and as the date of the ceremony approached, held a tisch, or bridal reception. During the tisch, the bride would go into the mikvah, or ceremonial bath, to be cleansed and then receive henna ink designs on her body both for protection and beauty.

There are many parallels between this betrothal period of Jewish couples and our relationship with Christ. Much like the bride price, Jesus paid a price for His people with His life on the cross (1 Corinthians 6:20; 7:23). Him having paid this price, believers have been called out and set apart for Jesus (1 Peter 2:9–10). Furthermore, Jesus said He was preparing a place for His followers in His Father's house (John 14:2–3). Ephesians 5:26–27 and 1 Corinthians 6:11

tell us that Jesus' blood shed on the cross washes believers like the mikvah cleanses the Jewish bride. The Holy Spirit protects believers and marks them as belonging to Christ much like the henna ink applied to the bride during the tisch (John 14:17; 16:13–15; Ephesians 1:13–14).

The second stage of a traditional Jewish wedding is nissuin, or the marriage, when the bride and groom are committed to one another. It begins with a ketubah, or contract outlining the rights and responsibilities of the couple to each other, being signed and witnessed. Then the groom places a veil over the bride during the bedeken, or veiling ceremony. He then prepares the chuppah, or canopy, under which the ceremony will take place. When the bride arrives under the chuppah, she encircles the groom three times to remind the people of God's three-time promise to betroth His people to Himself forever in Hosea 2:19–20. The groom places a ring on the bride's finger stating, "Behold, by this ring you are consecrated to me as my wife according to the laws of Moses and Israel." Seven blessings (Sheva Brachot) are then recited reflecting themes of Jewish marriage and God's role in that. The ceremony ends with the breaking of glass. The couple then gets ten to twenty minutes of time alone together during the Yichud. Finally, there is a reception filled with dancing, eating, and entertaining the couple. During the reception two glasses of wine are poured into one for the couple to share representing their two lives blending together into one.

The second stage of Jewish weddings also has many parallels to the believer's relationship to Christ. The ketubah for believers is the new covenant. Christ then clothes us in "the garments of salvation... [and] the robe of righteousness" like the groom covers his bride with the veil during the bedeken (Isaiah 61:10). The chuppah represents the couple creating a new life and home together, but the four sides are open to the community, just like our life with Christ is supposed to be openly shared with those around us (Matthew 28:19–20; Acts 1:8). The wife receiving the ring as an outward symbol of her relationship to her husband is similar to the Christian receiving the Holy Spirit as a seal guaranteeing our inheritance (Ephesians 1:13–14). Similarly, the words spoken during the ring ceremony echo Christ's words that all believers belong to Him in John 17:9–10. The Seven Blessings are prayers glorifying God for His creation and work in the couple's life, just as we are called to glorify God for His work in and around us (Romans 15:4–6; 9–12). Finally in Revelation, we see a wedding reception like none on earth with feasting and singing and joy unbridled. Just as the bride and groom are to become one as symbolized in the glass of wine, so too are we to have the mind of Christ and be one as His church (1 Corinthians 2:16; Romans 12:5; 15:5–6; Ephesians 5:29–32).

There are many encouraging parallels to explore when looking at God's use of the marriage metaphor when describing His desired relationship with His people. An understanding of traditional Jewish wedding ceremonies only enhances our understanding of that metaphor and thereby builds our understanding of who God is and how He works with His people.

CAN A DIVORCED PERSON REMARRY?

Most people who are divorced remarry "Can a divorced person remarry?" is, legally, yes. But is it a good idea? And what does the Bible say?

The Bible only mentions three situations in which a divorced person may remarry. It is believed that Matthew 5:32 gives a person permission to remarry if their marriage ended due to adultery on the part of their spouse. First Corinthians 7:39 says that a widow or widower may remarry; combined with 1 Corinthians 7:11, this would extend to someone who remained celibate after divorcing for non-adultery or abandonment reasons. First Corinthians 7:11 goes on to say that if a divorced couple has not remarried others, they are encouraged to reconcile and remarry each other. If there are other circumstances in which remarriage is endorsed by God, the Bible doesn't mention them.

But should a divorced person remarry, even if the Bible specifically allows it? In 1 Corinthians 7:40, Paul says, "Yet in my judgment she is happier if she remains as she is…" that is, divorced and unmarried. Is this advice to the Corinthians, who were about to face severe religious persecution? Or is it universal?

If any divorcee chooses to remarry, it would at least be a good idea to address the causes of the divorce. The more often a person is married, the more likely any subsequent marriage will fail. A change in spouse doesn't change the heart. In fact, previously married people are 90% more likely to divorce in subsequent marriages.

Why does this matter? Because it shows that people who are divorced and remarry have not dealt with the issues that caused the first divorce. It could be judgment in choosing a spouse, communication skills, trust, or just the inability to commit to another person the way God designed us to. Until and unless those personal issues are addressed and resolved, even the most innocent divorcee should seriously reconsider before marrying again.

Here's another sobering statistic: children who have divorced parents are 40% more likely to divorce their own spouse. But children whose divorced parents remarry other people are 91% more likely to divorce. While witnessing a divorce up close compels children to become ambivalent about the worth of commitment in their own relationships, realizing that a partner can be easily replaced more than doubles that ambivalence.

Those who are eager to remarry after a divorce are caught up in a lie that is propagated by both secular society and Christian culture—that marriage is the standard and singleness is inferior. Jesus is clear that singleness can be a gift (Matthew 19:12). Paul says that singleness can mean a life free to serve God in a way married couples cannot (1 Corinthians 7:32-35). One's marital status should reflect the Lord's leading, not fear of loneliness or the judgment of people who don't interpret Scripture properly.

Can a divorced person biblically remarry? Not if they committed adultery during their first marriage. Not if they divorced their spouse for trivial reasons. And not if they haven't resolved the issues that fed their first divorce. Still, God is gracious and forgiving. If we seek His kingdom first, it may be that He will restore the year's bad judgment and emotional trauma have stolen.

WHAT IS THE BIBLICAL VIEW ON DIVORCE AND REMARRIAGE?

The Bible gives very scant guidance regarding remarriage after a divorce.

In Matthew 19:9, Jesus says, "And I say to you: whoever divorces his wife, except for sexual immorality, and marries another, commits adultery." Some interpret this to mean that if a marriage ends because of infidelity on the part of one party, the innocent party is free to remarry.

Divorce and remarriage is also allowed if a blameless spouse was sent away, remained single, and the divorcing spouse died. First Corinthians 7:39 says, "A wife is bound to her husband as long as he lives. But if her husband dies, she is free to be married to whom she wishes, only in the Lord." Like a widow, if a man or woman remained faithful to their wedding vows before and after the marriage, death releases them.

Finally, remarriage is more than allowed—encouraged, even—between the couple that originally divorced (1

Corinthians 7:11). Deuteronomy 24:1-4 gives the stipulation that neither party marry someone else in the meantime. A reconciled marriage is one of the great blessings God grants those who follow Him.

There are more verses that explain when it is not appropriate to remarry after divorce. Matthew 5:32 says that if a man divorces his wife, he causes her to commit adultery (assuming that she remarried). Mark 10:11 says that any man who divorces his wife and remarries commits adultery against his first wife. And 1 Corinthians 7:11 says that if a wife leaves her husband, she should remain unmarried or reconcile to her husband.

The Bible is clear that remarriage is permitted to the innocent spouse whose divorce was due to adultery and to the faithful spouse who is released by death. But Scripture does not command people to remarry. First Corinthians 7:32-35 was written to Christians who were about to go through horrible persecution, but the words are still worth considering today:

I want you to be free from anxieties. The unmarried man is anxious about the things of the Lord, how to please the Lord. But the married man is anxious about worldly things, how to please his wife, and his interests are divided. And the unmarried or betrothed woman is anxious about the things of the Lord, how to be holy in body and spirit. But the married woman is anxious about worldly things, how to please her husband. I say this for your own benefit, not to lay any restraint upon you, but to promote good order and to secure your undivided devotion to the Lord.

The grounds for divorce given in the Bible feel incredibly strict. Tenderer hearts wish to allow remarriage for abused spouses, people who became believers after the divorce, and even Christians who have grown more mature in their faith. It is entirely possible that God will call those in such circumstances to remarry. Such specifics just aren't found in Scripture.

WHAT DOES IT MEAN THAT A WIFE IS SUPPOSED TO BE A HELPMEET/ HELP MEET?

The word "helpmeet" comes from the King James translation of Genesis 2:18: "And the LORD God said, It is not good that the man should be alone; I will make him a help meet for him." Over time "help meet" has morphed into one word that has come to be a Christian phrase for the role a woman fulfils in marriage. "Helpmeet" is also sometimes used as a synonym for "helpmate."

The ESV puts Genesis 2:18 this way: "Then the Lord God said, 'It is not good that the man should be alone; I will make him a helper fit for him.'" The NKJV has "a helper comparable" and the NIV uses "a helper suitable." The Hebrew word translated as "helper" is `ezer. In other parts of the Bible `ezer is used in reference to God's help, giving a clue to the kind of help that a wife gives (Deuteronomy 33:26; Psalm 20:2; 70:5; 115:9–11; 121:1). Being created in the image of God, a wife does not offer the kind of help a tool or an animal gives; her help is similar to the kind that God can give. The Hebrew word translated as "meet" or "fit" or "suitable" (neged) means "a counterpart" or "a mate" or "corresponding to" or "in front of" or "parallel to." This refers to something that is different from Adam, but is within the same purpose. The help is suitable, or fitting, because it corresponds to him. The concept of a helpmeet gives the picture of parallel lines: the husband and wife are not the same, but they follow the same path. Eve was made as a suitable companion to Adam. A wife being a helpmeet is an honourable and valued position, not one of inferiority.

God deemed everything He created "good", but after God created Adam He said that it was not good that he should be alone. Humans are social beings. God created Eve for Adam as a companion, as a mate, and as someone to complement him. As a woman, Eve had different characteristics and strengths from Adam that would aid him in fulfilling God's calling on his life. Adam could not "Be fruitful and multiply and fill the earth and subdue it, and have dominion over the fish of the sea and over the birds of the heavens and over every living thing that moves on the earth" (Genesis 1:28) on his own. And God, knowing Adam's character intimately, was able to make just the right woman in disposition, personality, and character to help him.

God created man and woman to work together as a team in His purpose for them, complementing one another in our various strengths and weaknesses. In a societal sense, both men and women are essential and valuable. When speaking specifically of marriage, God created a husband and wife to live together as one flesh (Genesis 2:24). Of course, not every man or woman will get married, and Paul talks about the good opportunities for serving God that come with celibacy (1 Corinthians 7:7–9). However, within the marriage the concept of a wife as a helpmeet essentially means that a wife should be walking in a way that would help her husband and not hinder him.

HOW IS THE CHURCH THE BRIDE OF CHRIST?

Several places in the Bible use the imagery of marriage to describe the relationship between Christ and the church.

Ephesians 5 uses the example of Christ's relationship to the church as instructive for marriage. Ephesians 5:23 talks about the husband being head of the wife (leader of the family) and compares that to Christ being the head of the church. Similarly, verse 24 notes that the church is to submit to Christ; the comparison here involves the submission of a godly woman to her loving husband.

Ephesians 5:25-27 describes how Christ loved the church and gave His life for it.

Likewise, a husband is to love His wife unconditionally and without limit. Christ loves the church as He loves Himself (Ephesians 5:28-30). Likewise, a husband is to love his wife as himself, considering their marriage as "one body."

The Ephesians 5 passage on marriage summarizes, "let each one of you love his wife as himself, and let the wife see that she respects her husband" (v. 33). Mutual love and respect form the basis for a God-honouring marriage. Likewise, Christ's love for the church and the church's love and respect for Christ form the basis for a God- honouring church.

Second Corinthians 11:2 offers a similar look at Christ as the groom and the church as the bride of Christ. Here Paul writes, "For I feel a divine jealousy for you, since I betrothed you to one husband, to present you as a pure virgin to Christ." Paul uses this analogy to show his love for the Corinthian believers, serving in the role as a spiritual father, offering the church at Corinth to Christ as the groom.

In addition, the New Jerusalem described in Revelation 21 is called "a bride." It is the place where all of God's people will dwell here with Him for all eternity. The beauty of this "bride" is stunning.

Though the New Jerusalem is not the bride of Christ, it complements Ephesians 5 in showing the loving relationship between Christ and His people. The marriage relationship, rightly practiced, reflects many of the ways Jesus loves His people, the church, as its husband.

DOES THE BIBLE TALK ABOUT A CHRISTIAN STAYING SINGLE?

The examples of the apostles show us that some were single (Paul, for example), some were married (Peter, for example), and some we aren't told their marital status. Paul wrote the Corinthians that some people were gifted for singleness and some for marriage (1 Corinthians 7:7).

Paul wrote to the Corinthians during a time of trouble and persecution. He said, "I think that in view of the present distress it is good for a person to remain as he is. Are you bound to a wife? Do not seek to be free. Are you free from a wife? Do not seek a wife. But if you do marry, you have not sinned, and if a betrothed woman marries, she has not sinned. Yet those who marry will have worldly troubles, and I would spare you that" (1 Corinthians 7:26–28).

Marrying is not a sin. Staying single is not a sin. God wants His people to live a life devoted to Him, regardless of marital status. Both marriage and singleness have advantages and disadvantages. Marriage is a gift and is highly lauded in the Bible. Marriage is the foundational family unit, a beautiful depiction of Christ and the church, the only appropriate venue for sexual activity, the means of procreation, and intended as a life-giving and encouraging partnership (Genesis 2:24; Ephesians 5:22–33; Hebrews 13:4). It involves great joy as well as great pain and sacrifice.

Singleness is also a gift; it is not a lesser status. Staying single does not imply that there is something wrong with the unmarried person or that he or she is somehow incomplete. In fact, if anything, the Bible seems to speak of singleness as a high calling. There can be great focus, freedom, and joy in being single. There can also be isolation and deep longing. Neither marriage nor singleness will shield a person from the hardships of life. Neither is a superior status or somehow more holy or Christian than the other. Again, the important thing for all is honouring God, which can be done married or single.

To seek God's guidance for your life, ask Him for wisdom (James 1:5). Also consider Romans 12:2: "Do not be conformed to this world, but be transformed by the renewal of your mind, that by testing you may discern what is the will of God, what is good and acceptable and perfect." Attempt to approach life with a godly perspective and ask Him to both guide and provide.

Whether married or single, God's will for you is to: "Rejoice always, pray without ceasing, give thanks in all circumstances; for this is the will of God in Christ Jesus for you" (1 Thessalonians 5:16–18).

WILL SEX BE PART OF HEAVEN?

In Matthew 22:23-33, the religious teachers called the Sadducees asked Jesus a question concerning the law involving marriage. In response, Jesus stated in verse 30,

"For in the resurrection they neither marry nor are given in marriage, but are like angels in heaven." His answer clearly notes that marriage will not take place in heaven. Because sex is designed for marriage, then sex will also not take place in heaven.

People in heaven will be "like angels in heaven." This does not mean people turn into angels, but that people in heaven will likewise exist as beings who focus on worship and service to God.

Further, from God's perspective, sex is a unifying part of the marriage relationship and is not meant for any other relationship. When a person is married, "'Therefore a man shall leave his father and his mother and hold fast to his wife, and the two shall become one flesh'? So they are no longer two but one flesh" (Matthew 19:5-6). This need for oneness as a married couple will no longer be necessary in heaven. The Lord Himself will satisfy every need and desire.

Some argue that sex will take place in heaven because sex is a part of who we are, not what we do. In other words, there will be gender roles of male and female in heaven because that is part of our identity. However, this is distinct from saying people will participate in sexual activities in heaven. There will be no need for these activities if God provides complete contentment and every desire is already satisfied.

People appear to still have a body in heaven, but do not perform the same activities or roles associated with our human bodies on earth. Instead, we will worship God, "And I heard every creature in heaven and on earth and under the earth and in the sea, and all that is in them, saying, 'To him who sits on the throne and to the Lamb be blessing and honour and glory and might forever and ever!'" (Revelation 5:13), feast with the Lord (Isaiah 25:6; Matthew 8:11; Luke 22:30), live together with other believers, celebrate (Revelation 19:9) serve God (Matthew 4:10), and exist in amazing surroundings (Revelation 21—22).

ARE SEXUAL DESIRES INHERENTLY SINFUL?

Sexual desires are not inherently sinful. In the paradise of the Garden of Eden before sin entered the world, God said, "It is not good that the man should be alone; I will make him a helper fit for him" (Genesis 2:18). In a perfect and sinless world, God created Adam with a need for connection with a fellow human. God then provided for this need by fashioning a woman whom Adam recognized as "bone of my bones and flesh of my flesh" (Genesis 2:23). Upon seeing the woman, Adam had a visceral reaction, recognizing a fellow human with whom he could fellowship in a unique way. Genesis 2:25 records, "the man and his wife were both naked and were not ashamed." Being together and desiring human connection was nothing to be ashamed of and constituted no sin.

In Song of Solomon, God provides an intimate illustration of the love and sexual desire between a husband and wife. In Song of Solomon 5:16 the wife proclaims about her husband, "he is altogether desirable." Later in Song of Solomon 7:10 she states, "I am my beloved's, and his desire is for me." Both the husband and wife feel sexual desire for the other. In the middle of this poetic ode to love, God pronounces a blessing over their sexual relationship. In Song of Solomon 5:1, the "Others" declare, "Eat, friends, drink, and be drunk with love!" This pronouncement echoes what God said in the Garden of Eden in Genesis 1:28, "And God blessed them. And God said to them, 'Be fruitful and multiply and fill the earth.'" God is the creator of sex and He has blessed the sexual desires and sexual union of married couples.

Unfortunately, sin has entered our world and corrupted the good and holy desires God created, twisting them in ways God did not intend. The situations in both Genesis and Song of Solomon speak of desire within committed, monogamous, heterosexual relationships. Those desires are to be encouraged and indulged. Problems arise, however, when our sexual desires are indulged outside those parameters.

When Paul wrote to the Corinthians he explained that "if they cannot exercise self- control, they should marry. For it is better to marry than to burn with passion" (1 Corinthians 7:9). Here Paul explained that self-control is necessary when it comes to sexual desire. The desire itself is not sinful, rather the way in which we handle the desire determines whether or not we sin. In fact, Paul reiterates, "if his passions are strong… let them marry—it is no sin. But whoever is firmly established in his heart… having his desire under control, keep her as his betrothed, he will do well" (1 Corinthians 7:36–37). The passionate desire itself is not sinful. The options then are to marry and indulge that desire in the way God intended or to keep that desire under control, refraining from marriage, and exercising self-control over one's thoughts and actions.

Proverbs 5 contrasts the goodness of sexual desire within marriage against the wickedness of indulging those desires outside of marriage. When speaking of the wife, Proverbs 5:19 says, "Let her breasts fill you at all times with delight; be intoxicated always in her love." However, it continues with a warning, "Why should you be intoxicated, my son, with a forbidden woman and embrace the bosom of an adulteress? He dies for lack of discipline, and because of his great folly he is led astray" (Proverbs 5:20, 23). Sexual desire for his wife was encouraged, but desire for another woman was not to be indulged. Instead the son was called to exercise self- discipline. This same principle can be applied for any sexual desire we may feel. Misdirected desires can lead us into sin if we indulge them by continually thinking on them, lusting in our thoughts, or engaging in sexual activity outside of God's parameters. But sexual desire within God's parameters for sex is nothing to be ashamed about; in fact, it is encouraged.

Our sexual desires are ultimately meant to help us understand God more fully. God often refers to Himself as a husband and to His people as a wife (Hosea 2:16; Isaiah 54:6). Paul writes, "'Therefore a man shall leave his father and mother and hold fast to his wife, and the two shall become one flesh.' This mystery is profound, and I am saying that it refers to Christ and the church" (Ephesians

5:31–32). God passionately desires to be united with His people and for His people to passionately desire Him. Jesus prayed for this kind of unity in John 17 when He said, "I in them and you inme, that they may become perfectly one, so that the world may know that you sent me and loved them even as you loved me" (John 17:23).

The physical desire for sexual intimacy with a fellow human is meant to be an illustration of the spiritual zeal for unity with God that we're to hope for. Our sexual desires are meant to draw us closer in relationship to God, whether that is through relying on His Spirit to develop in us self-control, or through enjoying the passionate intimacy of a monogamous marriage that reflects God's passion for His people and their returned passion for Him. In this way, sexual desire is a great gift from the Lord for which we can give Him thanks and praise.

SHOULD CHRISTIANS DATE OR MARRY NON-CHRISTIANS?

Should a Christian marry an unbeliever? In a society where people can have hundreds of online friends from all over the world, it can still be difficult to find close, personal relationships in real life. Sometimes it feels like a miracle when we meet someone with whom we really connect—someone who likes us, likes spending time with us, and makes us feel appreciated. When that magic happens, it can be easy to gloss over differences that don't seem to have any immediate bearing on the personal relationship. More and more Christians who want to marry are finding themselves willing to overlook differences in faith.

It is possible to have a loving relationship with an unbeliever. But it is also inevitable that such a close connection will draw the believer away from God (1 Corinthians 15:33). Dating or marrying an unbeliever will seemingly solve a lot of issues, such as loneliness, perceived cultural pressure to marry, and the desire to live life with someone else. But the solution comes with a very high cost.

Some will cite things such as child-rearing decisions, financial decisions, church participation, and holiday traditions as areas of tension between a believing spouse and an unbelieving spouse. Certainly these might be areas of tension, but that could be true in most any marriage regardless of faith. The biblical prohibition against marrying an unbeliever is not intended simply to spare believers an uncomfortable marriage or marital disagreements. Believers in Jesus Christ are spiritually alive. They are citizens of heaven (Philippians 3:20). They know and have a growing relationship with God. They are called to be living sacrifices and to live their lives as unto God (Romans 12:1–2; Colossians 3:1–17). Unbelievers are still slaves to sin (Romans 6:6– 11). The whole foundation of life for believers and unbelievers is opposed. Willingly becoming one flesh with someone who is spiritually dead is ill-advised.

Also consider what type of witness marrying an unbeliever gives. How can we profess to love God yet disobey His clearly stated command? How can we profess to love a spouse yet be apparently unconcerned with his or her eternal salvation? How can we relegate our relationship with Jesus Christ to mere religion and act as if it is a cultural barrier that could be overcome?

When the single life gets hard, and marrying a non-Christian looks like the only choice, it's imperative to decide what is most important. If following Christ and serving Him in any circumstance is paramount, the decision is easy—don't be unequally yoked (2 Corinthians 6:14); look forward to what God is accomplishing (Romans 8:28); and trust that God's blessings are better than we can imagine (Ephesians 3:20). Rely on Him to meet your needs; He is sufficient for every need we have. Choosing to date or marry a non-Christian is rejecting God as a primary influence. It is clearly declaring "God is not enough." And it may possibly be abandoning God's plan for a godly relationship He has waiting in the wings.

SOUL TIES – WHAT DOES THE BIBLE SAY?

A "soul tie" is a mystical bond between two people. The phrase is used to describe love at first sight or an obsession that is so strong it feels like two souls are entwined. The concept is also used to justify an ungodly relationship.

The Bible does not allow for the existence of a "soul tie."

Genesis 2:24 says that a married couple become "one flesh," not one soul. Jesus said that there is no marriage in heaven (Matthew 22:30), which would not be the case if people were joined in their souls.

What we think of as a "soul tie" actually may have more to do with the sense of smell. The closer two people are, the more they get used to and develop an addiction to the hormones the other naturally emits. Dopamine, norepinephrine, serotonin, oxytocin, and vasopressin all combine to make us "feel" in love. God allowed this so that married couples develop even closer relationships.

Another possible source of the feeling of a "soul tie" is a psychological obsession. Romantic obsessions are based on what we think of the other person. This does not necessarily have anything to do with reality; and it's foolish to expect someone to be what we want them to be rather than who they are.

A close relationship can feel like a "soul tie." But even the closest relationship based on personality and mutual love does not mean the two souls are entwined. Sometimes the concept of "soul ties" is used as an excuse to indulge in an ungodly obsession. Feeling like your soul is tied is not an excuse to stay in a relationship that is unbiblical. And it is not some insurmountable force that constrains us to sin. It's just an excuse to stay in sin. Instead of using "soul ties" as a rationalization, we should deal with the sin (1 John 1:9).

The only soul we are tied to is that of the Holy Spirit. If He indwells us, He is entwined with our soul. All other relationships, no matter how close, are a combination of physiological response to chemicals, mutual interest, natural affinity, or sinful obsession.

PRINCIPLES OF MARRIAGE 3

- ➤ A successful marriage pivots on knowledge-knowing, understanding and practising God's principles.

- ➤ Always success is dependent on how much knowledge we know and apply rather than how we may feel about something.

- ➤ God's original creation of man and woman was to exercise equal authority and dominion.

- ➤ Power and authority individually is not leadership. But authority and power is true leadership in its servant nature.

- ➤ The power of marriage's success is directly proportional to the amount of knowledge and wisdom and time invested in it.

- ➤ The power of a success planning is application of God's moral principles and values as stipulated in the scriptures.

The foundation for building a successful marriage is built on application of the fruits of the Holy Spirit which are:

> Charity (or Love)

> Joy.

> Peace.

> Patience.

> Kindness.

> Goodness.

> Longanimity.

> Mildness.

> Faith.

> Modesty.

The power of a successful marriage is also built on the gifts of the Holy Spirit one has which are:

1. The Word of Knowledge

2. The Word of Wisdom

3. The Gift of Prophecy

4. The Gift of Faith

5. The Gifts of Healings

6. The Working of Miracles

7. The Discerning of Spirits

8. Different Kinds of Tongues

9. The Interpretation of Tongues

The other important aspects that make a successful marriage are:

- Financial stability

- Adaptability

- Submission

- Respect

- Empathy

- The ability to work through challenge

- The ability to give and receive

- Ability to communicate with honesty

- Emotional stability

- Being lead with reason, knowledge and understanding not emotions

- Similar backgrounds

- Making agreed and reasonable choices and decisions

- Leaving your parents' home to join your husband's home is a foundation principle of marriage.

- A wife and a husband relationship is the primary human relationship.

- A man is a logical thinker but a woman an emotional feeler thus understanding each other is needed.

- The emotional language is one language that is heard by a woman's experience

- Men can be itinerant. Women require strong security roots

- Men are tend to stable and level off.

- Women tend to be guilt prone but men tend to be resentful

➢ A husband and a wife must be each other's best friend

➢ Openness and transparency are true signs of friendship

WHAT DOES IT MEAN THAT GOD IS LOVE?

The Bible teaches that God loves us, yet also teaches that God is love. First John 4:7-9 reveals, "Beloved, let us love one another, for love is from God, and whoever loves has been born of God and knows God. Anyone who does not love does not know God, because God is love. In this the love of God was made manifest among us, that God sent his only Son into the world, so that we might live through him."

In the original Greek used to write the New Testament, there is more than one word for love. The Greek word agapos, often referred to as agape love, is the word used in 1 John 4. It is used when speaking of an unconditional love. This love of God is boundless.

God does not only give love; He is the source of love. As the Creator of all things (Genesis 1:1), He is the One who created love. It is because of His love that we are able to love. As 1 John 4:19 notes, "We love because he first loved us."

The fullest expression of God as love was through the Son,

Jesus Christ. God created us, sustains us, and has revealed Himself to us through Jesus. John 1:14 declares, "And the Word became flesh and dwelt among us, and we have seen his glory, glory as of the only Son from the Father, full of grace and truth."

Among the most famous of Bible passages on love is 1 Corinthians 13. In these verses we find a picture of God's love expressed in poetic terms that displays many of the aspects of God's love toward us. We are told, "Love is patient and kind; love does not envy or boast; it is not arrogant or rude. It does not insist on its own way; it is not irritable or resentful; it does not rejoice at wrongdoing, but rejoices with the truth. Love bears all things, believes all things, hopes all things, and endures all things. Love never ends." (1 Corinthians 13:4-8).

Further, John 3:16 teaches, "For God so loved the world, that he gave his one and only Son, that whoever believes in him should not perish but have eternal life." God has made clear that His love through the Son of God, Jesus, provides an opportunity for those who believe to spend eternity with Him. It is God's desire for us to enjoy His love both in this life and for all eternity.

The Bible is also clear we have done nothing to deserve God's perfect love. Romans 5:8 shares, "but God shows his love for us in that while we were still sinners, Christ died for us." Even when Jesus knew we would fail and even before we were born, He gave His life as the ultimate expression of His love.

God is love. He created love, created us to love Him, and has extended His love to each of us. Our challenge is to accept His great love (Ephesians 2:8-9) that we may experience His love in our lives today (John 10:10) and for eternity (John 3:16).

HOW DOES GOD DEMONSTRATE HIS LOVE FOR US? WHY DOES GOD LOVE US?

This profound question finds its answer in the very nature of God Himself. First John 4:8 teaches that, "God is love." Not only does God love; love is part of His essential nature. Love is who God is, therefore He cannot but love.

Do we deserve His love? Romans 5:8 clearly teaches, "God shows his love for us in that while we were still sinners, Christ died for us." We had not even been born yet, and God was already at work to provide a way for us to spend eternity with Him (John 3:16). Jesus even noted that He is preparing a place for those who love Him (John 14:3) where we will dwell in His presence forever.

There are limitless expressions of God's perfect, unconditional love for us. One of these is the fact that He created us. Colossians 1:16 says, "All things were created through him and for him." This includes every person who has ever lived. John 1:3 adds, "All things were made through him, and without him was not anything made that was made."

God also shows His love for humanity by sustaining our lives. Colossians 1:17 teaches, "And he is before all things, and in him all things hold together." First Peter 1:5 notes believers are those, "who by God's power are being guarded through faith for a salvation ready to be revealed in the last time." Second Timothy 1:12 adds, "I know whom I have believed, and I am convinced that he is able to guard until that Day what has been entrusted to me."

God has revealed His love through sending His only Son Jesus Christ to provide salvation for those who believe. John 3:16 observes, "For God so loved the world, that he gave his only Son, that whoever believes in him should not perish but have eternal life." His salvation provides inexpressible joy, "Though you have not seen him, you love him. Though you do not now see him, you believe in him and rejoice with joy that is inexpressible and filled with glory, obtaining the outcome of your faith, the salvation of your souls" (1 Peter 1:8-9).

God reveals His love through salvation. Ephesians 2:8-9 instructs, "For by grace you have been saved through faith. And this is not your own doing; it is the gift of God, not a result of works, so that no one may boast." Salvation is God's free gift to those who will receive it, an expression of love that includes eternal life.

God reveals His love through the calling and gifts He has given us. Ephesians 2:10 shares, "For we are his workmanship, created in Christ Jesus for good works, which

God prepared beforehand, that we should walk in them." First Corinthians 12:7 adds, "To each is given the manifestation of the Spirit for the common good."

God reveals His love by making believers part of God's family. As 1 John 3:1 declares, "See what kind of love the Father has given to us that we should be called children of God; and so we are."

God reveals His love for believers particularly by preparing an eternal home with Him. John 14:2-3 promises, "In my Father's house are many rooms. If it were not so, would I have told you that I go to prepare a place for you? And if I go and prepare a place for you, I will come again and will take you to myself, that where I am you may be also."

Many additional examples could be provided to show how God loves us, but the only adequate reason to explain why God loves us is found in His very nature. He is love, and His love for us as His created beings ultimately brings glory to His name.

WHAT THINGS CAN HELP IF I DON'T FEEL LOVE FOR GOD?

No one feels love for God until he or she is born again. We are spiritually dead until we receive salvation in Jesus Christ (Ephesians 2:1–10). First John 4:10 says, "In this is love, not that we have loved God but that he loved us and sent his Son to be the propitiation for our sins." We only love God because He loved us first (1 John 4:19). Once we are born again, nothing can pry us from God's love (Romans 8:38–39).

Even so, we may not always "feel" love for God. We know that emotions ebb and flow over time, including our feelings toward God. It is important to remember that even when we don't feel it, God still loves us. And, even when we don't feel it, we can still choose to trust God, choose to act, and choose to have faith in God. Our relationship with God is not based on feelings and circumstances, but on His truth and on faith.

God is all forgiving and compassionate toward you (2 Corinthians 1:3). Remember, He did not respond to you and your feelings, but you responded to His love and the truth of His action to send His Son Jesus Christ for you (John 3:16). Ours is a reaction, a response to His great love. Because He never changes (Hebrews 13:8), we can seek to be consistent in our reaction to His love.

When you don't feel love for God, keep on choosing to love God. Dive into His Word, the Bible, for encouragement. You will see the lengths He has gone to reach you and establish a relationship with you. The Psalms and 1 John may be particularly pertinent.

Keep praying. Tell God of your troubles, give Him praise for the truths you read about in His Word, and ask for His help.

Continuing to go to church is important. The community of believers is meant for mutual encouragement and building up (Hebrews 10:24–25). Being with others who also believe God and are seeking to live for Him can help renew our love for God.

Taking communion is also important. It is a remembrance service, bringing to mind Jesus' goodness to us (1 Corinthians 11:23–26). This physical act of remembrance can help renew our feelings of love for God.

Remind yourself of God's past faithfulness as a way to renew your love for Him. If you keep a journal, or simply remember these times, you can look back at times that God has been good to you, shown mercy and compassion, rescued you from a difficulty, and the like. You can also begin to pay attention to the ways you currently see God at work and record those in a journal. This will help you to focus on God's love for you and help renew your love for Him (Philippians 4:8).

You might also consider finding a Christian mentor, someone who is mature in the faith and who has evident joy in the Lord. Ask this person to advise you and walk with you.

Having mountain-top experiences with God is great and wonderful and gives us touchstones to return to as reminders of His greatness. But we all know there are valleys near every mountain, and plains leading to it all. Our walk with God is not in the clouds, but here on earth—an earth that has been corrupted by sin. It is natural to feel discouraged at times, and even to lack love for God at times. But when we feel this way, we can remind ourselves of His truth— through reading the Bible, through praying, through fellowshipping with other believers. Love is not a constant high, but a daily choice. God's love is steadfast and something on which we can always rely.

When you don't feel love for God, know that God hears your heart, and hears your prayers. Ask Him for help. David wrote, "In my distress I called upon the LORD; to my God I cried for help. From his temple he heard my voice, and my cry to him reached his ears" (Psalm 18:6). Hebrews 4:14–16 and Hebrews 10:19–23 tells us we can draw near to God in full faith because Jesus has opened a way for us.

If your distance from God continues to grow, please seek the assistance of a reputable Christian counsellor. A Christian counsellor can uncover with you the root of your difficulties and help to formulate a strategy to grow closer to God in your unique circumstances.

Know this: God is pursuing you with as much passion and love as He did when you first met Him.

Paul ends his letter to the Ephesians with a lovely prayer we share with you here (Ephesians 3:14–21): "... I bow my knees before the Father, from whom every family in heaven and on earth is named, that according to the riches of his glory he may grant you to be strengthened with power through his Spirit in your inner being, so that Christ may dwell in your hearts through faith—that you, being rooted and grounded in love, may have strength to comprehend with all the saints what is the breadth and length and height and depth, and to know the love of Christ that surpasses knowledge, that you may be filled with all the fullness of God. Now to him who is able to do far more abundantly than all that we ask or think, according to the power at work within us, to him be glory in the church and in Christ Jesus throughout all generations, forever and ever. Amen."

HOW DOES SOMEONE LOVE GOD?

The more you know God, the easier it is for you to love Him—just as with human relationships. When you know the deeper intricacies of a person, it only helps you to appreciate and love him/her more (Psalm 34:8). So, what does it mean to love God? There are a few practical ways to love God and grow in your love for Him on a daily basis.

At the core, loving God means that we put Him first in every area of our lives. Jesus said that the greatest commandment is: "you shall love the Lord your God with all your heart and with all your soul and with all your mind and with all your strength" (Mark 12:30; Deuteronomy 6:5). God needs to be our number one priority. As we focus on Him, we are not swayed as easily by the things of this world. We are better able to love Him not just in our words but in our actions. Additionally, as we love God, He helps us to better love other people (Mark 12:31).

One way we show God love is by worshipping and praising Him, and Him alone (Luke 4:8). The book of Psalms gives us insight as to how we can give God love through our worship, praise, and thanksgiving toward Him (e.g., Psalms 8, 19, 23, 24, 67, 99, 117, and 150). Psalm 100 says: "Make a joyful noise to the LORD, all the earth! Serve the LORD with gladness! Come into his presence with singing! Know that the LORD, he is God! It is he who made us, and we are his; we are his people, and the sheep of his pasture. Enter his gates with thanksgiving, and his courts with praise! Give thanks to him; bless his name! For the LORD is good; his steadfast love endures forever, and his faithfulness to all generations."

If we want to love God better, we need to develop a love for His Word. God's Word teaches us about His character and it helps us to desire God, His righteousness, and His kingdom (Psalm 42:1; 119:105; Matthew 6:10). We find out that God is the source of all that we need: "Whom have I in heaven but you? And there is nothing on earth that I desire besides you. My flesh and my heart may fail, but God is the strength of my heart and my portion forever" (Psalm 73:25–26). By reading God's Word and spending time in prayer, we get to know His voice and His heart.

When we love God, we obey what He commands (John 14:15, 23; 15:10; 1 John 5:3). This obedience is not rooted in merely rote religious requirements; it is rooted in the fact that we know how much God loves us, so we naturally desire to please Him (Psalm 40:8). We cannot love both the world and God simultaneously (1 John 2:15), but when we truly know God and experience His love for us, we willingly choose to love Him back. Like Mary of Bethany, we desire to listen to what He is saying (Luke 10:39). As

1 John 4:19 says: "We love because he first loved us."

DOES GOD LOVE ME?

We know that God is love (1 John 4:8). We know that God loves the world (John 3:16). But does God love us as individuals? Does He love me, a sinner? Yes! Scripture is full of affirmations of God's love for individuals.

In the Old Testament, we are not shown merely a history of a people group. We meet individual characters, ones with whom God spoke and interacted. Moses, Joseph, Jonah, Job, David, Esther, Ruth, Jabez, Hagar, and more. God cared about these individuals, some of whom were not even Israelites.

In the New Testament, we see God's love take on skin. Salvation is the biggest demonstration of God's love for each of us (1 John 3:16). Jesus humbled Himself not only by taking on human flesh, but by allowing Himself to be brutally murdered for sins we committed (Philippians 2:5-8). He did this with joy (Hebrews 12:2). And He did it while we were still dead in our sins (Romans 5:6- 11; Colossians 2:13). We did not impress God or cajole Him into saving us. Salvation is completely from His heart of love. Jesus became sin that we might become righteous; He granted us new life (2 Corinthians 5:17, 21). He saved us for a purpose. We are called God's masterpiece (Ephesians 2:8-10). Part of that purpose is to share the love of Christ with others.

One beautiful picture of that love is Jesus washing His disciples' feet. It was a task for a lowly servant to scrub the mud-caked feet of house guests. After doing it, Jesus said, "A new commandment I give to you, that you love one another: just as I have loved you, you also are to love one another. By this all people will know that you are my disciples, if you have love for one another" (John 13:34- 35). Jesus was interested in showing love not only to His disciples, but to other people. He healed many; He provided food for the hungry; He spoke to the outcasts of the day, even a Samaritan woman (John 4). Jesus loved people on an individual basis. His ministry was not publicly broadcast, but carried out one- on-one. He chose a group of twelve disciples, an inner circle of three. He spoke to the individuals He healed. He did not exclude those who were not Israelites, but shared His love with whoever would receive.

Perhaps one of the most touching passages in the Bible is John 17, which records what is sometimes called the High Priestly Prayer. In it, Jesus prayed for His disciples. He also prayed for future believers – us. Before His crucifixion we were on Christ's mind. Not in a negative way or a blaming way. He thought about us and prayed "that they may all be one, just as you, Father, are in me, and I in you, that they also may be in us, so that the world may believe that you have sent me. The glory that you have given me I have given to them, that they may be one even as we are one, I in them and you in me, that they may become perfectly one, so that the world may know that you sent me and loved them even as you loved me. Father, I desire that they also, whom you have given me, may be with me where I am, to see my glory that you have given me because you loved me before the foundation of the world. O righteous Father, even though the world does not know you, I know you, and these know that you have sent me. I made known to them your name, and I will continue to make it known, that the love with which you have loved me may be in them, and I in them" (John 17:21-26). Jesus wants us to be united with one another, to be united with Him, to be with Him, to know Him, and to experience His love. This is not a prayer aimed at the world or at a group of nameless faces. It is a prayer about individuals.

Reading God's Word is an excellent way to discover His love for us. Look at some of what He says below:

For you formed my inward parts; you knitted me together in my mother's womb. I praise you, for I am fearfully and wonderfully made. Wonderful are your works; my soul knows it very well. My frame was not hidden from you, when I was being made in secret, intricately woven in the depths of the earth. Your eyes saw my unformed substance; in your book were written, every one of them, the days that were formed for me, when as yet there was none of them. (Psalm 139:13-16)

But even the hairs of your head are all numbered. Fear not, therefore; you are of more value than many sparrows. So everyone who acknowledges me before men, I also will acknowledge before my Father who is in heaven ... (Matthew 10:30-32)

The thief comes only to steal and kill and destroy. I came that they may have life and have it abundantly. (John 10:10)

As the Father has loved me, so have I loved you. Abide in my love. If you keep my commandments, you will abide in my love, just as I have kept my Father's commandments and abide in his love. These things I have spoken to you, that my joy may be in you, and that your joy may be full. (John 15:9-11)

For you did not receive the spirit of slavery to fall back into fear, but you have received the Spirit of adoption as sons, by whom we cry, "Abba! Father!" The Spirit himself bears witness with our spirit that we are children of God, and if children, then heirs—heirs of God and fellow heirs with Christ, provided we suffer with him in order that we may also be glorified with him. (Romans 8:15- 17)

What then shall we say to these things? If God is for us, who can be against us? He who did not spare his own Son but gave him up for us all, how will he not also with him graciously give us all things? ... No, in all these things we are more than conquerors through him who loved us. For I am sure that neither death nor life, nor angels nor rulers, nor things present nor things to come, nor powers, nor height nor depth, nor anything else in all creation, will be able to separate us from the love of God in Christ Jesus our Lord. (Romans 8:31-32, 37-39)

Therefore be imitators of God, as beloved children. And walk in love, as Christ loved us and gave himself up for us, a fragrant offering and sacrifice to God. (Ephesians 5:1-2)

The Lord is not slow to fulfil his promise as some count slowness, but is patient toward you, not wishing that any should perish, but that all should reach repentance. (2 Peter 3:9)

He who has an ear, let him hear what the Spirit says to the churches. To the one who conquers I will give some of the hidden manna, and I will give him a white stone, with a new name written on the stone that no one knows except the one who receives it. (Revelation 2:17).

HOW CAN I HAVE INTIMACY WITH GOD?

The question of perceived intimacy with God is an interesting one. Many Christians who feel that they do not have intimacy with God actually do have intimacy with Him, but they are misinterpreting a lack of emotion for lack of God's presence. There's nothing wrong with feeling emotional about God, but those feelings should not be relied upon as a proof of His presence. We know from experience that some people are more emotional than others, and that emotions are not always consistent. Thankfully, God's love and presence do not depend on anything so changeable.

The proof of God's intimacy with every believer is evident in Scripture. Because of our faith in Christ, we are righteous before God (2 Corinthians 5:21; Jeremiah 33:16; 1 Corinthians 1:30) and we know that He is intimate with the righteous (Proverbs 3:32). In His High Priestly Prayer, Jesus described the intimacy He has with believers, saying "I made known to them your name, and I will continue to make it known, that the love with which you have loved me may be in them, and I in them" (John 17:26). He spoke to His disciples about how the Father and the Son make a home with those who love Him (John 14:23). Nothing is more intimate than making a home with someone.

God's intimacy with His children is a fact, and our knowledge of it is based on faith in His promises, not on an internal sense of His presence, or on a swell of emotion or lack thereof. We do know that God desires obedience, and that the one who loves Him will keep His word (John 14:23). But that obedience is a result of our intimacy with God, rather than something we do to woo Him closer to us. He is a proactive God; He loves proactively—as the Scripture says, "while we were still sinners, Christ died for us" (Romans 5:8). He has promised never to leave us or forsake us (Hebrews 13:5-6).

Sin will always make a believer feel unhappy, but this is not because God has walked away—it is because of our intimacy with Him that we feel unhappy in those times. His Spirit dwells in us, and when we drag Him through sin, He doesn't like it and makes His unhappiness known. This is why Paul tells Christians not to grieve the Holy Spirit of God (Ephesians 4:30). If we did not have intimacy with God, and He was truly far from us, we would not feel His displeasure when we sin. We are always in an intimate relationship with God. But, just as in a marriage, if one spouse hurts another, it can cause brokenness and pain. Ask forgiveness, and a loving spouse will return without holding a grudge. A believer's relationship with God is the most forgiving relationship there is—the moment we return to Him, He forgives and loves, without bitterness or resentment. "As far as the east is from the west, so far does he remove our transgressions from us? As a father shows compassion to his children, so the LORD shows compassion to those who fear him. For he knows our frame; he remembers that we are dust" (Psalm 103:12-14).

True intimacy with God is the situation of every believer, but even in human relationships, intimacy is not always pleasant: the most severe wounds always come from the most intimate relationships, from being vulnerable with those we love. God places Himself in a position of vulnerability by choosing to be intimate with fallen, broken creatures. And, at times, His love creates pain for us as well. Like a loving Father, He disciplines us, and it can be disappointing and confusing when that pain arrives. But it is also a sign that both His love and His intimacy with us are real (Proverbs 3:11-12; Hebrews 12:5-11), and we can take great comfort in that.

WHAT DOES 'PERFECT LOVE CASTS OUT FEAR' MEAN?

The Bible says that "perfect love casts out fear" (1 John 4:18). What is perfect love and how exactly does perfect love cast out fear? To truly understand this verse, we must look at the passage leading up to it. John writes, "In this the love of God was made manifest among us, that God sent his only Son into the world, so that we might live through him. In this is love, not that we have loved God but that he loved us and sent his Son to be the propitiation for our sins. ... By this we know that we abide in him and he is in us, because he has given us of his Spirit. And we have seen and testify that the Father has sent his Son to be the Saviour of the world. Whoever confesses that Jesus is the Son of God, God abides in him, and he in God. So we have come to know and to believe the love that God has for us. God is love, and whoever abides in love abides in God, and God abides in him. By this is love perfected with us, so that we may have confidence for the Day of Judgment, because as he is so also are we in this world. There is no fear in love, but perfect love casts out fear. For fear has to do with punishment, and whoever fears has not been perfected in love" (1 John 4:9–18).

In this verse, the Greek for the phrase "perfect love" is teleios agape and "perfected in love" is teleioo agape. "Perfect" here is referring to that which is mature or complete. It is not just a love that is whole, but it is a love that has been completed. The Greek word used here for love, agape, is the highest of the four Greek words for love. It refers to a self-sacrificial, unconditional love, full of good will toward its object. To say that "perfect love casts out fear" is to say that "mature, completed, unconditional love that wants the best for you casts out fear."

God is the only one who has such love. The Bible says that

God is love, and all of our love stems from Him (1 John 4:7–8), and as such God is the only one who has perfect love. The perfect love of God has been "completed" on the cross when God sent His only Son to die for our sins, so that we may live in relationship with Him, and now there is no condemnation for those who are in Christ Jesus (Romans 8:1). It is by grace we are saved through faith, and there is nothing we have done to earn our salvation, nor is there anything we must do to maintain our salvation; we are secure in Christ (Ephesians 2:8–10; John 3:16–18; 10:29).

First John 4:18 says that "fear has to do with punishment." Judgment is coming at the end of our lives, but for the Christian, there should be no fear of punishment in his or her relationship with God. God's love has made a way for our sins to be atoned for. As 1 John 4:10 explains, Jesus is the propitation for our sins, or satisfaction for the penalty our sins deserve from God. The Christian's sins have been paid for on the cross and there is thus no fear of judgment—"perfect love casts out fear" (1 John 4:18).

It is not only that we need not fear eternal judgment; we can also approach God without fear now because of His perfect love. His love is not dependent upon us following the Law or "doing the right thing" all of the time. His love is a constant in our lives. We know that in Jesus Christ our sins have beenforgiven and we know that God is a God of grace, eager to cleanse us and restore us to full fellowship with Him when we sin (1 John 1:8–9). Hebrews 10:19–23 says,

"Therefore, brothers, since we have confidence to enter the holy places by the blood of Jesus, by the new and living way that he opened for us through the curtain, that is, through his flesh, and since we have a great priest over the house of God, let us draw near with a true heart in full assurance of faith, with our hearts sprinkled clean from an evil conscience and our bodies washed with pure water. Let us hold fast the confession of our hope without wavering, for he who promised is faithful." Hebrews 4:16 says that we can "with confidence draw near to the throne of grace, that we may receive mercy and find grace to help in time of need" (Hebrews 4:16). There is no fear in the love of God because we know that He is always ready to forgive, always ready to show mercy.

John says that the one who fears "has not been perfected in love." The non- believer is afraid of God because he knows that he faces judgment for his sins (John 3:18), but the believer knows that God is full of mercy and love, and that he is promised eternal life in paradise with Him (John 3:16). But even believers sometimes have fear, especially when we find ourselves in sin. But this fear is simply a result of immaturity in faith. So how does one mature in love?

In the passage in 1 John, right after stating that God is love, John says "whoever abides in love abides in God, and God abides in him. By this love is perfected with us" (1 John 4:16–17). We are perfected in love by abiding in love. When we spend time with God, learning who He is, and understanding His character as revealed in the Bible, we become mature in love because we know who Love is. We know that God is faithful when we are faithless (2 Timothy 2:13). We know that He disciplines us in love (Hebrews 12:6). We know that He walks alongside us in hardships and trials, using them to mature and sanctify us (James 1:2–4; Romans 5:2–5). We know that He teaches us truth and equips us with all we need for life (2 Timothy 3:16–17; 2 Peter 1:3). We know that He is with us (Matthew 28:19–20; John 14:15–17; Ephesians 1:13–14; Hebrews 13:5–6). We know that "he who is in you is greater than he who is in the world" (1 John 4:4). We know that Jesus has defeated sin and death and that God has given us victory through Him (1 Corinthians 15:54–58). We know that Jesus isreturning (Philippians 3:20; Titus 2:13; Acts 1:11; James 5:8). We know that nothing can ever separate us from God's love (Romans 8:38–39; John 10:29). We learn that God has given us His spirit to live in us, not one of fear, but one of power, and of love, and of a sound mind, so that we do not have to fear (2 Timothy 1:7).

When we come to know God we know that we can trust Him. We learn that He has done more than enough to earn our trust. So now we do not need to fear,

1)   because we know that Jesus has born our judgment on the cross (2 Corinthians 5:17–21), and 2) because we know that the God of love is the God of this universe and He is on our side.

PRINCIPLES OF MARRIAGE 4

- ➤ God is love.

- ➤ God created mankind in His image.

- ➤ Without God we cannot achieve anything and without us God will not achieve His intention for our creation.

- ➤ God created both man and woman to receive His love.

- ➤ God creates and created by speaking.

- ➤ The primary purpose for our creation is to praise, worship and love God.

- ➤ Loving and having intimacy with God means knowing and understanding God's ways

- ➤ Knowing God is the starting place to acquire knowledge and wisdom.

We must have a vertical relationship with God first then have an intra-personal relation (a good relationship with yourself) and lastly have an interpersonal relationship or horizontal relationship (A healthy relationship between man and woman).

IS THERE A DIFFERENCE BETWEEN FORNICATION AND ADULTERY?

Traditional dictionary definitions of fornication and adultery generally define fornication as sexual relationships between unmarried people and adultery as a sexual relationship between two people in which at least one of the people involved is married to someone else.

In the King James and New King James Versions of the Bible, fornication is a word used in the Old Testament in relation to sexual sins. It is also used to talk about idolatry. For example, in 2 Chronicles 21, the fornication or sexual immorality of the people included involvement in idolatry with Baal. In Ezekiel 16, fornication was repeatedly used to describe the idolatry of God's people. In the New Testament, fornication is often the translation of the Greek word porneia that includes sexual immorality of many kinds, both adultery and other sexual sins. In Matthew 19:9, this word, translated "sexual immorality," is used as a case in which God permits divorce.

In the Bible, adultery is used in the normal sense as sexual relations outside of a person's marriage. While the Bible also uses the word figuratively to speak of the "spiritual adultery" of God's people, adultery is typically used in reference to an extramarital relationship. Mentioned 22 times in the New Testament, it is used only once in reference to spiritual adultery (Revelation 2:22). All other times it is mentioned in its normal sense as a sinful practice.

Adultery is also specifically listed as prohibited in one of the Ten Commandments (Exodus 20). This made it a practice especially condemned in Jewish culture. Most notable was the affair of King David with Bathsheba that caused much trouble. Yet even in this case, David later repented and received forgiveness from God, despite the consequences (Psalm 51). Likewise, John 7:53-8:11 describes a woman caught in adultery whom Jesus forgives.

In the New Testament, adultery is likewise condemned. It serves as one of the only reasons given that provide opportunity for divorce (though not required). Jesus mentioned this in Matthew 5:32 and 19:9. James 2:11 noted both adultery and murder as sin before God.

Both fornication and adultery are considered sinful in Scripture. However, the Bible is also clear that God provides forgiveness for these sins, and offers new life to those who will trust in Him.

IS FORGIVENESS AVAILABLE FOR ANY AND ALL OF MY SIN?

Believers and non-believers alike are often under the impression that the Christian God forgives, but only up to a point. There are certain sins that we think are "too sinful" or "too bad" to be forgiven by God. Sometimes this mind-set comes from a misunderstanding of Scripture, and other times it comes from an internal feeling on the part of the sinner. In either case, the Bible makes it very clear to the believer that there is literally no sin, including any sin committed before or after acknowledging Jesus as Lord, that will destroy our relationship with Him and place us outside His loving grace (Romans 8:38–39).

The only sin that cannot be forgiven is the sin of unbelief—for obvious reasons. If you do not believe that you need to be forgiven, how can you receive forgiveness? If you do not believe that God exists, how can you have a relationship with Him? If you do not accept Jesus, who is the only way of salvation, as Saviour, how can you be saved? Jesus mentioned the "unpardonable sin" which is blasphemy against the Holy Spirit (Mark 3:22–30; Matthew 12:22–32) and indicates continued unbelief. The sin is unpardonable not because of a lack in God's love or ability, but because the pardon is unwelcomed by the unbeliever.

Jesus' sacrifice is fully sufficient to cover any sin we commit. The doctrine of the atonement explains this. Hebrews 10:4–14 says, "For it is impossible for the blood of bulls and goats to take away sins. Consequently, when Christ came into the world, he said, 'Sacrifices and offerings you have not desired, but a body have you prepared for me; in burnt offerings and sin offerings you have taken no pleasure. Then I said, "Behold, I have come to do your will, O God, as it is written of me in the scroll of the book."' When he said above, 'You have neither desired nor taken pleasure in sacrifices and offerings and burnt offerings and sin offerings' (these are offered according to the law), then he added, 'Behold, I have come to do your will.' He does away with the first in order to establish the second. And by that will we have been sanctified through the offering of the body of Jesus Christ once for all. And every priest stands daily at his service, offering repeatedly the same sacrifices, which can never take away sins. But when Christ had offered for all time a single sacrifice for sins, he sat down at the right hand of God, waiting from that time until his enemies should be made a footstool for his feet. For by a single offering he has perfected for all time those who are being sanctified." Second Corinthians 5:21 says, "For our sake he made him to be sin who knew no sin, so that in him we might become the righteousness of God."

Sometimes, unbelievers resist relationship with God because they fear they will have to follow a list of laws as a kind of payment for the forgiveness God offers. Nothing could be further from the biblical doctrine of salvation. God desires truth in the inner man. He wants us to come into the light, and to be honest with Him and with ourselves (Psalm 51:6; 1 John 1:9). For all of us, this includes the acceptance of our inability to obey that list of laws, and the admittance of our inability to change ourselves, or even our inability to desire change in ourselves. It is simply impossible for us to earn God's forgiveness by anything we do (Romans 5:6–11; Ephesians 2:1–10). We do not serve a God that needs to be appeased with good works. Instead, God works to produce good things in us as we face the truth about ourselves, and depend on Him (Psalm 3:5–6; John 15:3–5; John 7:38; John 3:16–18; Ephesians 2:8–10). The forgiveness of salvation is completely apart from our works. Good works result from having been made new in Christ at salvation (2 Corinthians 5:17) and the continued work of the Holy Spirit in our hearts (Philippians 1:6; 2:12–13; Galatians 5:16–26).

Once we have been saved by God's grace through faith in Jesus it can be easy to be trapped by the lie that God requires proof of salvation in exchange for forgiveness or in order to remain forgiven. For example, if a person struggles habitually with some addictive sin, like alcoholism or lust, they can be tempted to believe that God forgives them while they are doing well, but that they need to restore His forgiveness each time they fall into sin in order to stay saved. If the sin is habitual and a continual struggle, this pattern can lead the person to start thinking "maybe I'm not really saved after all, because wouldn't I have victory over this sin if I were?" It is good to examine oneself and be sure you really have placed your faith in Jesus and that you are actively seeking to follow Him. But the truth is that every believer struggles against sin. Even after salvation, we still have the flesh, which wars against the new, sanctified spirit within us. Even the Apostle Paul dealt with this (Romans 7:14–25). It does not preclude God's forgiveness. Forgiveness is a state of being, not a thing we have to access each time we sin. Jesus' sacrifice for us on the cross was "once for all" (Romans 8:1; Hebrews 10:10).

The distinction to be made is that of justification and sanctification. When we are saved, we are completely forgiven for every sin—past, present, and future. We are declared completely righteous before God. However, during this lifetime, we are being functionally made righteous. We become more like Jesus, and we sin less. We do still ask God to forgive our sins (1 John 1:8–9), but this is about spiritual growth and recognizing how our sins hurt the heart of God. It is not that we lose and regain salvation with each sin. And God is "faithful and just to forgive us our sins and to cleanse us from all unrighteousness" (1 John 1:9). There is no sin that cannot be forgiven in Jesus. His work on the cross is fully sufficient. The price has been paid. Accept His wonderful gift today.

HOW DO I RECEIVE FORGIVENESS FROM GOD?

All people have sinned (Ecclesiastes 7:20; Romans 3:23) and stand in need of God's forgiveness. How do we receive forgiveness from God?

The Bible clearly teaches that Jesus is the source of forgiveness of sins: "Let it be known to you therefore, brothers, that through this man forgiveness of sins is proclaimed to you" (Acts 13:38)

How can we be forgiven from our sins? First, we acknowledge we are sinners. First John 1:8 teaches, "If we say we have no sin, we deceive ourselves, and the truth is not in us."

Second, we confess our sins to God. First John 1:9 teaches, "If we confess our sins, he is faithful and just to forgive us our sins and to cleanse us from all unrighteousness." God desires to forgive us (2 Peter 3:9) and has made a way for us to be forgiven through Jesus Christ alone (John 14:6; Acts 4:12).

Third, we trust in Jesus Christ by faith. Ephesians 2:8-9 teaches, "For by grace you have been saved through faith. And this is not your own doing; it is the gift of God, not a result of works, so that no one may boast." We do not earn forgiveness through our works. Instead, we believe in Jesus by faith and receive His free gift of eternal life.

How can you believe in Jesus Christ and receive forgiveness of sins? Romans 10:9 teaches, "If you confess with your mouth that Jesus is Lord and believe in your heart that God raised him from the dead, you will be saved." Salvation happens when you believe Jesus is Lord and accept that He died for your sins and resurrected from the dead.

But what if you are already a Christian? Being a Christian is not a license to sin, but does mean that sins you commit after becoming a believer are also forgiven. But when Christians do sin, we should still confess those sins and turn from them. First John 1:9 applies to Christians, too. As Christians we are called to live righteously (John 14:15; 15:9-11; 1 Peter 1:13-16) for God and His purposes for our lives (Romans 12:1-2).

Do you want to place your faith in Jesus Christ as your Saviour and receive His forgiveness and free gift of eternal life? You can do it now. There is no special prayer you must pray to do so. However, the following prayer is one you can use to ask for forgiveness and accept salvation:

"Dear God, I realize I am a sinner in need of forgiveness. I can never make up for my sins against you through my own actions or reach heaven by my own good deeds. But you have provided a way for me to receive forgiveness. Right now I place my faith in Jesus Christ as God's Son who died for my sins and rose from the dead to give me eternal life. Please forgive me of my sins and help me to live for you. Thank you for accepting me and giving me eternal life."